GOD
COMES
OUT

The Center for Lesbian and Gay Studies in Religion and Ministry

Pacific School of Religion
1798 Scenic Avenue
Berkeley, California 94709
Phone: (800) 999-0528
Fax: (510) 849-8212
www.clgs.org

GOD COMES OUT

A QUEER HOMILETIC

Olive Elaine Hinnant

Foreword by Thomas Troeger

THE
PILGRIM
PRESS
Cleveland

For Thomas Troeger, who saw the seed,
for Rose Annette Liddell, who watered it,
for Linda Glenn, who pruned it of commas,
and for Sue Lawson Cawthon, who kept me planted
on this earth, thank you.

The Pilgrim Press
700 Prospect Avenue
Cleveland, Ohio 44115-1100
thepilgrimpress.com

© 2007 by Olive Elaine Hinnant

All rights reserved. Published 2007

❀ Printed in the United States of America on acid-free paper that contains
   post-consumer fiber.

12 11 10 09 08 07   5 4 3 2 1

Library of Congress Cataloging-in-Publication Data
Hinnant, Olive Elaine, 1962-
    God comes out : a queer homiletic / Olive Elaine Hinnant.
       p.   cm.
    "The Center for Lesbian and Gay Studies in Religion and Ministry."
    Includes bibliographical references (p.   ).
    ISBN-13: 978-0-8298-1730-0 (alk. paper)
    1. Homosexuality – Religious aspects – Christianity. 2. Spirituality.
    3. Preaching.   I. Title.
    BR115.H6H56 2007
    251.0086'64 – dc22
                                              2007020717

Contents

Acknowledgments

My appreciation and thanks go to the preachers who gave permission to have their sermons reprinted in this book. From them we recognize what God is doing through lesbian, gay, bisexual, and transgendered people, and our allies. I also remember and want to thank the many who, by their faithful listening, shape preachers and the word they preach.

Preface to the Series

Gayatri Spivak, an important contemporary postcolonial theorist, en-titled her famous 1988 essay, "Can the Subaltern Speak?"[1] in order to ask whether the Indian people who lived under the colonial power of the West could ever truly speak in their own voices. In the end, she decides they could not because their representation in society was always crafted not by themselves, but by the dominant voices of the colonizers' discourse, in which the colonized masses existed primarily as abstractions to be pointed to, not as real people with their own lives and views. They were the objects of social discourse, never its subjects. While the differences between the formerly colonized people of India and those who today identify as part of the lesbian, gay, transgender, bisexual, or queer communities are vast, the situation of being the objectified, silenced "Other" within the discourses of the dominant culture is remarkably similar.

Over the past century particularly, as debates over the moral and civil status of sexual minority groups have raged in churches, halls of government, courts, professional associations, and city streets, the loudest and often the only voices heard were those of the dominant heterosexual majority. Whether those voices were raised in denigra-tion or, more rarely, in support, bisexuals, lesbians, gay men, and transgender people themselves were often visible only as silent ab-stractions within the violent logic of homophobia and heterosexism. They were allowed little or no public voice; whatever knowledge they possessed about their own situations was deemed inadequate, naive,

---

1. Gayatri Chakravorty Spivak, "Can the Subaltern Speak?" in Cary Nelson and Lawrence Grossberg, eds., *Marxism and the Interpretation of Culture* (London: Macmillan, 1988).

biased, or simply irrelevant to the debate about them. The elite experts of the dominant heterosexual group, the doctors, lawyers, politicians, clergy, and scholars, established themselves as the only reliable sources of knowledge about those "others" whom their "expert witness" often condemned to silence — or worse.

Fortunately, within the last fifteen years much of this enforced public silence has been shaken off by the concerted action of sexual minority groups themselves and their growing number of supporters. Significant legal and political victories upholding the equal civil rights of LGBTQ people along with the courageous determination of increasing numbers of LGBTQ people to be "out" and visible in society together seem to be slowly turning the tide of public ignorance and fear. However, full social and cultural acceptance of LGBTQ people will not be achieved by legal and legislative remedies alone. Only when other important social institutions open their doors to enlightened discussion will some of the final obstacles to full equality really disappear. Religion remains one of the major arenas in which ignorance about and hostility toward sexual minorities still dominate many groups. In most of these cases, LGBTQ people remain abstractions or objects, often portrayed only through the fantasies of the dominant group itself, rather than real people who can speak authoritatively about their own lives. Many faith communities continue doggedly to listen only to the characterization of LGBTQ people proposed by their own heterosexual leaders, assured, it seems, that no religious or spiritual understanding could possibly be found within the gay, lesbian, transgender, bisexual, or queer communities themselves. Such an assumption could not be further from the truth.

The very struggle for dignity in a hostile world, especially a hostile religious world, has brought with it remarkable religious knowledge and astonishing spiritual strength to LGBTQ people of faith. LGBTQ people of faith can be found in every religion, congregation, and faith community in the world. Because of their lived experience both within and outside of established communities of faith, LGBTQ people know what it means to stand courageously for who they are and for what they believe. They also know how to create and nurture family in the midst of rejection; how to care for and love friends even through illness and death; how to hang onto faith, even in the presence of persistent evil; and how to support each other faithfully and grow spiritually in the face of hatred and derision. Moreover, they know the deeply liberating joy of the good news preached to those who are oppressed, and they know how full of grace an embodied sexuality can really be. All of these gifts and graces of the spirit and more, all of this knowledge and strength are desperately needed today, not only by other marginalized populations, but perhaps even more so by faith communities at large in the dominant culture.

This book series, sponsored jointly by the Center for Lesbian and Gay Studies in Religion and Ministry at Pacific School of Religion and by The Pilgrim Press, is designed precisely to make more widely available the stories, insights, new knowledge and religious gifts of many within the transgender, queer, lesbian, gay, and bisexual communities — not only to support those who might be walking similar paths, but also to awaken the wider religious world to the spiritual genius of people it has all too often denigrated and rejected. For Jews and Christians, after all, there is strong precedent for attending to such people; as Jesus, quoting Psalm 118, pointed out, "The stone that the builders rejected has become the cornerstone" (Mark 12:10). The time has come for faith communities to listen and to learn from new voices and new perspectives.

The value of LGBTQ people voicing the truths of their own lives is nowhere more vital than in the realm of Christian preaching. By simply embodying their identities in the pulpit, LGBTQ preachers speak, as Olive Elaine Hinnant observes, a "bold word even before we open our mouths." By acknowledging the gifts of LGBTQ preachers and straight allies through the collection and analysis of ten powerful sermons, Hinnant in this book begins to shape a queer homiletic that can serve both LGBTQ people of faith and their straight allies. Through discussions of the role of coming out in fashioning queer identity, the liberating reading of the Bible by outsiders, the development of queer theology, and the dynamics of preaching itself, Hinnant's work lays the foundation for a robust queer homiletic. Illustrating each element with richly evocative sermons from a variety of people, mostly lesbian or gay but some straight, mostly out but some closeted, Hinnant weaves a rich fabric of poetic analysis and creative homiletic. This important volume combines a thoughtful study of the recent history of homiletics in America with a theologically informed evocation of a queerly attuned homiletic practice to produce a powerful and informative challenge for preaching about a God who comes out and a people called to be out with God and each other.

MARY A. TOLBERT
Executive Director
Center for Lesbian and Gay Studies
in Religion and Ministry
Pacific School of Religion

Foreword

I remember when I was learning Greek in seminary and I discovered that the word we translate "reveal" means literally in the original "uncover." Something that is hidden comes into view. Revelation (apocalypse) is an act of uncovering, a disclosure of truth that we had not seen before.

The primary meaning of "revelation" in Greek returned to me again and again in reading Olive Elaine Hinnant's *God Comes Out*. The book is a revelation, or more accurately, a series of revelations uncovering truths that most of our churches have hidden or ignored. Some of the revelations are very painful, such as the damage and distortion caused by fear-driven theologies against same-gender-loving people. Hinnant's work makes clear that the church needs to face up to its role in perpetuating the abuse of people whom God loves and accepts just as they are. But she also offers many other revelations that are filled with hope. She calls us to acknowledge the interfusion of our sexual energies and the divine vitalities. She draws out the queer character of the creator whose image all of us bear, and she celebrates the spiritual enrichment of embracing the varieties of human sexuality with which God has gifted our communities.

Revelation is not something that happens all at once. Instead, it is very much like the process of coming out, of self-identifying as a lesbian, gay, bisexual, or transgendered person. It is not a singular event, but something that unfolds over time. I found very helpful Hinnant's quotation from George Takei, who describes coming out through "the metaphor of a long, narrow corridor which is dark at first, then there are little glimmers of light coming in, then it starts to widen, and there's a window opening. And you peek out, and you see some possibilities. And then there are doors ajar, and you might step out briefly and then come back in. So, it is a long process. It's not as the word 'out' suggests — a sudden decision and you step into another world."

These powerful words call to mind the last several decades of social and theological upheaval. Groups that have been historically marginalized have found their voices and have insisted on the recognition of their full, God-given humanity. They have made it clear that they deserve a place at God's table with everyone else. Nothing changed instantly as they began to speak. The church did not all of a sudden "step into another world" of equality and justice. Instead, it was much more like walking through a "long, narrow corridor which is dark at first," with the light breaking through only partially, until we saw and began to claim more and more of the new life to which the Spirit beckoned us. In many cases the church initially resisted and rejected the new light, but over time it became a revelation, an uncovering of what we had not seen before.

I see Hinnant's work as part of this continuing revelatory process. Like biblical revelation, her book expands what we know about God, human beings, and their interactive relationship. I have no doubt there will be readers who condemn and dismiss her writing by pointing to isolated passages of Scripture and claiming that what she writes contradicts the Bible. But in truth what Hinnant writes is profoundly biblical because it centers itself so securely in the divine/human relationship, and it empowers us to live more fully the two greatest commandments, love of God and love of neighbor.

There will be other readers who will welcome this book, not only for its wisdom and compassion, but also for its practical suggestions about how to initiate liberating conversation about sexual differences. Pastors especially will gain deep insight into how preaching a fully inclusive gospel can draw our communities into a more faithful realization of the reign of God. By including ten sermons and closely analyzing them, Hinnant offers us an important work in homiletics.

She demonstrates again and again how preaching is above all a theological act, a giving witness to the grace and the love, the justice and the compassion, the wonder and the glory of God.

Hinnant offers us a vision of what the human community can be when it takes with utter seriousness that every one of us bears the image of God. That is a theological conviction central to the gospel, but it is also one of those truths that keeps getting hidden by our fear of difference and the rationalizations we develop to justify our rejection and mistreatment of others. By focusing on God as the creator and lover of human beings in all their varied richness, Hinnant never gets mired in the imbroglios of biblical interpretation that often choke our discussions of sexuality. Instead, she leads us to windows and doors where we see the light shining on the just and hospitable human community that God is calling us to create, a community that some welcoming churches are already beginning to gather.

Hinnant knows hers is a long-term project, and in the final chapter she humbly calls her book "only a beginning." But it is the beginning of a revelation that can empower preachers to bear witness to One whose persistent compassion is by the world's standards of bigotry and violence very queer indeed.

Thomas H. Troeger
Yale Divinity School and
Institute of Sacred Music

Chapter 1

The Problem

In the early part of the twentieth century, the great Jewish thinker Martin Buber rediscovered the mystical wisdom of eighteenth-century Hasidim. In Hasidic traditions the underlying command in life is to be "humanly holy." For example, when one Hasid is asked by another, "What is the most holy thing that your rabbi does?" he answers, "Whatever the rabbi is doing at that moment." On the basis of this mystical thought and his own personal experience, Buber came to describe as an "I-Thou" (as opposed to an "I-It") relationship any authentic interpersonal encounter that is characterized by mutuality, the recognition of the uniqueness of the other, and attentiveness. The experience that led Buber to this theological understanding of the Holy and humanity is recounted by his friend, Aubrey Hodes: "The key moment happened, when as a young professor, he was visited by an unknown young man. Buber was friendly and attentive but without 'being there' in spirit. After the conversation, Buber later learned that the young man who had come to see him had killed himself."[1]

---

1. Aubrey Hodes, *Martin Buber: An Intimate Portrait* (New York: Viking Press, 1971), 242. "What happened was no more than that one forenoon, after a morning of religious enthusiasm, I had a visit from an unknown young man, without being there in spirit. I certainly did not fail to let the meeting be friendly, I did not treat him any more remissly than all his contemporaries who were in the habit of seeking me out about this time of day as an oracle that is ready to listen to reason. I conversed attentively and openly with him — only I omitted to guess the questions which he did not put. Later, not long after, I learned from one of his friends — he himself was no longer alive — the essential content of these questions; I learned that he had come to me not casually, but borne by destiny, not for a chat but for a decision. He had come to me; he had come in this hour. What do we expect when we are in despair and yet go to a man? Surely a presence by means of which we are told that nevertheless there is meaning."

1

Chastened by this experience, Buber named this deeply intuitive sense of knowing and relating to another person the I-Thou. It is a critical concept for describing how sexual minorities should be referred to and thought of in religious dialogue.

For more than forty years mainline religious organizations within the United States and now, worldwide, have been engaged in a nasty, self-involved struggle regarding the lives of particular Christians, Jews, and those of other faiths — those ones who are also lesbian, gay, bisexual, or transgender (LGBT).[2] Typically, their contention has been that these two aspects of a person — faith and a nonheterosexual orientation — are not compatible, and therefore, an "issue," and a "problem." So, when debating membership, ordination practices, and union ceremonies, those whom the discourse is about are typically referred to as "the problem," "an issue" or "it." This worldwide controversy continues to create division in denominations because "the problem" will not go away. Indeed, if one were to search "religion" on the Internet, LGBT people will be found among Muslim, Buddhist, Hindu, Mormon, Jewish, Protestant, Catholic, Jehovah's Witness, and even Evangelical Christian communities. For as the LGBT community chants: "We're here, we're Queer, and we're not going away!"

The crux of this conflict came home to me in the arena of preaching when the pastoral relations committee of the church I was serving told me not to preach about "it" — meaning homosexuality. A review of my sermons would reveal that I had not been preaching about "it," even though I was hired as one who is also an out lesbian minister. The prohibition of preaching about "it" represented both an oppression of my sexual orientation and apparently a conflict for others about theology and God. Thus when I (or any other out LGBT clergy) preach, I

---

2. LGBT refers to lesbian women, gay men, and bisexual and transgender people. It is one term used to refer to people whose sexual practice is in the minority or those whose gender identity is fluid rather than fixed (also seen in a variety of forms: GLBTQ, LGBTQQI). This work focuses on the experience of persons who are either lesbian or gay men with the acknowledgment that bisexual and transgendered preachers and persons will want to bring their experiences to bear upon my work.

am perceived by some to *be* "it," the other, the homosexual, the "problem." However, I, together with my other LGBT brothers and sisters, am also a human being created in the image of God who reflects this particular difference to God's people. Both that we preach and that we are homosexual (or same-gender-loving) challenges many people's long-held images, beliefs, and ideas about who God is, thus making it difficult to hear a sermon without the stigma of preaching about "it." The discomfort, the newness, the challenge that out lesbian, gay, bisexual, and transgender clergy bring simply by their presence can cause well-meaning church members to call homosexuality an "issue," and to disrespectfully call a homosexual person an "it" rather than a mutual, relational "thou," as Martin Buber explained in his relational quality of dialogue.[3] When we objectify a person and reduce him or her to "it," we lose the human quality that is reflective of our Creator God.

Church historian and author Martin E. Marty, in his column M.E.M.O. in the *Christian Century*, writing about the debate over gay and lesbian clergy and same-sex blessings, said, "I wish we could start this one over, this time dealing with it not only as what Martin Buber would call an 'I-It' dispute but in a conversational 'I-Thou' form."[4] I believe it is not too late to begin such a relational approach. In preaching, we make a choice about how we communicate to listeners. Public communication through words to a general collection of people is best done in a conversational way that indicates a relationship. This means using an I-Thou form, rather than suggesting certain people, be they Jewish, LGBT, or fundamentalists, are "It" in relation — objects not people.

This idea of using Buber's understanding of dialogical relating in preaching is not new. English preacher and author Herbert H.

---

3. Martin Buber, *I and Thou: A New Translation, with a Prologue and Notes*, trans. Walter Kaufmann (New York: Touchstone, 1996), 53.

4. Martin E. Marty, "Ordained by Baptism," *Christian Century*, March 9, 2004, 55.

Farmer wrote about the use of the "I-Thou" dialogue for preaching in the 1960s:

> Preaching is the restoration of the fabric of the "I-Thou" world when it has been torn. God's approach to us is always through other persons, or, more generally, through history which is the sphere of persons in relationship.... God's I-Thou relationship with me is never apart from, is always in a measure carried by, my 'I-Thou' relationship with my fellows.[5]

Yet when it comes to personal relationships, the fabric of the church has been and continues to be torn apart by diverse expressions of sexuality. Treating people as objects or problems can cause a great deal of harm. Primarily, it cancels our relationship with God because that relationship is dependent upon our treatment of one another, as Buber pointed out. In his moment of realization after encountering the young man, Buber recognized the bond between humans and the choice to live. When a person is ignored or dismissed by another person, as Buber did the student, this diminishes both people as well as the Creator God who resides within us all.

Truly, while the presenting debate is about homosexuality, it is really about sex and our relationship to the Holy Other and the holy other (meaning our neighbor, or Buber's "Thou"). Our culture's dominant teaching about sex is that it is a relationship between one man and one woman within marriage and only for procreation. This pattern is argued on the basis of a certain interpretation of the Bible that includes cultural reinforcements such as the need for marriage to supply children and order and restraint in society. This interpretation assumes there is no other sexual practice within Scriptures, but that is not at all so.[6] The Scriptures are in fact full of diverse forms of family and familial relations. We seem willing to keep ourselves fooled by one

---

5. Herbert H. Farmer, *The Servant of the Word* (Philadelphia: Fortress, 1964), 23, 37.

6. Virginia R. Mollenkott, *Sensuous Spirituality: Out from Fundamentalism* (New York: Crossroad, 1992), 194.

narrowly defined practice of sexual expression. Why? What does this say about the majority who do not practice sexuality according to this dictum? What about our seniors who, for the most part, neither pro-create nor marry? Our formulas for sexual ethics are theoretical and do not match the realities of human lives where sex really matters. In-stead, our questions ought to be probing and profoundly reflective of sex where it is found and not how we think it is. How do we treat one another when it comes to sexual expression and commitment? How do we treat our primary intimate relationship — with or without a sense of the Sacred and the potential for good? We in the church and culture are in the messy middle trying to reconfigure a theology of sex that reflects our lives and faith in our Creator. Though we might say that homosexuality is rocking the church, it is really the larger topic of sexuality that is forcing us to be honest about who we are. Mean-while, LGBT preachers are giving a new image to the once-assumed straight God.

To put this in context, the church's current crisis of sexuality may be seen as through a kaleidoscope — real life situations that overlap, sharing colors and forms, but constantly morphing into more and more images. Certainly, there are endless stories of LGBT people at the in-tersection of Christian faith, a majority of them from the perspective of them being an "it," an "issue," or a "problem." Most of the stories come to light around votes on policy toward LGBT people, the ordi-nation of LGBT people, and the blessing of unions between couples. As the number of out clergy increases, subtle changes are occurring within church life — occasions that bring the straight God out of the closet.

A journalistic example reinforces the scope of the "problem": *Insight Magazine* carried an article: "The Mainline Churches Face a Great Divide."[7] Reporter John Powers briefly reviewed American mainline denominational history regarding hot-button social issues, including

---

7. John M. Powers, "The Mainline Churches Face a Great Divide," *Insight Magazine, The Washington Times*, December 23, 2003, 27.

the current one — homosexuality. Some of this attention, he reports, is the result of the consecration of Rev. V. Gene Robinson as the first openly gay bishop in the Episcopal Church on November 3, 2003. However, this is merely the tip of the iceberg. If one were to look at the last thirty years within any denomination, it would be obvious that this debate has been brewing both publicly and privately. Some say Robinson's ordination is the last straw for their participation in the Episcopal Church, but in fact this struggle has gone on for many decades and is not news. Also quoted in the *Insight* article is Deborah Caldwell, senior producer at Beliefnet.com, who has reported on the major Christian denominations for more than a decade. "Every Christian group in America right now has or is experiencing a cultural battle over homosexuality,"[8] Caldwell writes.

In yet another context, this one a seminary classroom, Catholic theologian and author Mary Hunt goes further in her analysis of the situation regarding sexuality and religion. In her class lecture she stated

> that virtually no religion in the world is without discussion on sexuality, whether it be homosexuality, heterosexuality or bisexuality, whether it be sexual abuse of children, or sex scandals in the church or teaching sexual values to teens. Public discussions, dialogue and debate about sexual issues are the new frontier.[9]

James B. Nelson, who has authored books in the area of Christianity and sexuality for thirty years, reminds us that there is an unfinished sexual revolution in the church despite efforts to repress and deny matters of sexuality.[10] The revolution is going nowhere until we see each person as God sees, as Thou, as a reflection of God in humanity.

---

8. Ibid.

9. Mary Hunt, "Same-Sex Love in American Religion," Summer School course, Iliff School of Theology, July 18, 2002, Denver, Colorado.

10. James B. Nelson, "Embracing the Erotic: The Church's Unfinished Sexual Revolution," *Reflections*, Yale Divinity School, New Haven, CT (Spring 2006): 18.

One of the ways we have attempted to solve the "problem" has been to try to find what causes people to be lesbian or gay. Yet this approach serves only to further negate the people who are lesbian or gay. Rather than being a problem to be solved, could we take the approach of learning to understand another difference about humanity and creation? Instead of searching for the causes of homosexuality, let us first find the causes of heterosexuality and then we will move away from seeing LGBT people as a "problem" or "issue" or an "it." Out LGBT preachers remind their listeners that acceptance of self is the hardest thing we have to do in life. While not all LGBT clergy have accomplished this, we have gone through quite a bit of soul searching and coming to terms with being rejected by others. That we accept ourselves and believe that God does also speaks volumes about the wideness of God's mercy. We, who have been the latest despised group in the church, are now in pulpits across America speaking a bold word even before we open our mouths.

If one were to pinpoint the pivotal public moment in the mainline churches about ordination of gays and lesbians, it would most likely be the United Church of Christ's ordination in 1972 of William R. Johnson as the first openly gay person in history to become a Christian minister. Lest anyone suggest that this discussion started suddenly, with his ordination, let us be clear that many denominational studies and reports predate this ordination.[11] Six years later, the first openly lesbian minister, the Reverend Anne Holmes, was also ordained in the United Church of Christ. By their public acclamation of homosexuality and gifts for ordained ministry, these individuals brought the

---

11. The Methodist Church and the Presbyterian Church produced booklets prior to the 1972 date. "Sexuality and the Human Community," Office of the General Assembly (1970), states "In November of 1966 the Council on Church and Society, The United Presbyterian Church in the U.S.A., took an action to launch a study on 'sexuality and the human community.'" Its task force was begun in 1967 and reported upon at the 1970 General Assembly. In the same time frame, the United Methodist Church General Board of Education published a study guide, "God and Human Sexuality" (1971). In London, SCM Press published Norman Pittenger's views on homosexuality in 1967, *Time for Consent? A Christian's Approach to Homosexuality.*

debate out of the closet and into the churches' purview in a personal
way. With their ordination, there was no denying the existence of
lesbian and gay persons in Christian ministry; thus, it was a major
turning point in American Christianity.

Thirty-five years into this historical shift in mainline Christian denominations with more out lesbian, gay, bisexual, and transgender
clergy in our pulpits, it is time we acknowledge the gifts of these
preachers. Our positive engagement from this study will shape a
homiletic that serves the LGBT community and its straight allies.
In addition, the aim of such study is to open the homiletical closet
door to the realities of lesbian and gay preachers and their sermons.
Two homiletical resources, one an encyclopedia of preaching and one
a history of preaching, published in 1995 and 2004, respectively, do
not include the presence of LGBT clergy or preachers.[12] This absence
exemplifies the invisibility of out LGBT preachers and in general the
treatment that LGBT church members, who listen to our sermons,
receive. When *The Concise Encyclopedia of Preaching*, in the section
on "Homiletics in North America" from 1960 to the present, does
not mention any LGBT voices, it fails to recognize the presence and
practice of LGBT members and ministers within the church. Furthermore, when the same resource lists tasks for the future of homiletics,
there is no mention of the church's crisis with regard to sexuality
or LGBT Christians.[13] While *A History of Preaching* does mention
"homosexuality," it appears in an example of William Sloane Coffin's
preaching on an "issue." The sermon is reported to be the best example
of Coffin's homiletic — his ability to preach prophetically on sensitive
personal matters.[14] It is not by a person from within the LGBT community, nor are there any other voices that might actually be from an
out sexual minority's perspective of the gospel. And this was published

---

12. O. C. Edwards, *A History of Preaching* (Nashville: Abingdon Press, 2004), and
William H. Willimon and Richard Lischer, eds., *Concise Encyclopedia of Preaching*
(Louisville: Westminster John Knox Press, 1995).

13. Willimon and Lischer, *Concise Encyclopedia of Preaching*, 248–52.

14. Edwards, *A History of Preaching*, 741.

in 2004, over three decades after the first ordinations of lesbian and gay ministers! This highlights the Christian church's ongoing silence regarding sexuality. By most people, including preachers, it is not even acknowledged.

But the denial of LGBT voices is only the beginning. Out lesbian, gay, bisexual, and transgender preachers face a unique homiletical challenge when their sexual orientation or gender identity dominates the way straight people hear their sermons. Framed another way, what homiletical tools and methods are necessary for out LGBT clergy to face privileged (i.e., heterosexual) congregations? Do those among us who preach in predominantly heterosexual contexts have different theological insights and biblical interpretations than straight clergy? What might a lesbian and gay homiletic look like? What does a lesbian or gay God look like? How does the process of coming out over and over again in our lives play itself out in our biblical study and exegesis? With the commonality of the coming out process among LGBT people — it being a transformational time in our personal lives — how is this applied to our theological understanding of God? These and other questions will be addressed in the creation of a transformational, prophetic homiletic for out clergy and our allies. Preaching in the face of the oppressions of heterosexism and homophobia presents challenges that current homiletical theories do not specifically address.

The homiletical landscape in North America in the last forty years has also had a fair amount of changes, though not as dramatic as the sexual revolution within the church. Nonetheless pulpits across America continue to experience change. For example, the homiletical field has moved from being a white male preacher's domain to a discipline shared by women, African Americans, Hispanics, Asian Americans, and those of many other ethnicities. While it is hotly debated, I believe our culture has shifted from modernism to postmodernism, which means, for example, that people generally question modernist values such as progress and rationality. They tend to believe that our reality is socially constructed, and that globalization has led to a lack of centralized power. The struggle for human rights in the 1960s has likewise brought an array of challenges. For instance, it was once common only for books of sermons by educated white men to be published. Two examples are *A Treasury of Great Sermons* — all by men, beginning with Jesus' Sermon on the Mount and ending with Norman Vincent Peale — and a collection of sermons by one author, *Phillips Brooks: Selected Sermons*. Even after the sixties, *The Riverside Preachers* (Fosdick, McCracken, Campbell, and Coffin) was published in 1978, and *The Twentieth-Century Pulpit*, vol. 2, appeared in 1981.[15] This last publication had one woman in its list alongside twenty men. Interestingly, two of the men listed in the second volume are now out gay men. Preaching as a discipline grew into its own theological category of study that overlapped with all other practical fields. The Academy of Homiletics was formed by men since there were very few women in pulpits then, even though the first woman was ordained in 1853.[16]

In 1982, a collection of Protestant, Catholic, and Jewish women's sermons was published, entitled *Spinning a Sacred Yarn*. It was one of the first collections of sermons solely by women, and was edited by Edwina Hunter and David Farmer. More books by women preachers followed, either as sermon compilations, such as *And Blessed Is She: Sermons by Women*, or as a single preacher's volume, such as *Mixed Blessings* by Barbara Brown Taylor. Among many collections of sermons by African American women preachers is one that includes original sermons in a historical overview. Bettye Collier-Thomas, author of *Daughters of Thunder: Black Women Preachers and Their Sermons, 1850–1979*, gives overdue attention to the voices of black women preachers.[17] All four books' content and courage

---

15. Daniel A. Poling, ed., *A Treasury of Great Sermons* (New York: Greenberg, 1944); William Scarlett, ed., *Phillips Brooks: Selected Sermons* (New York: E. P. Dutton, 1949), Paul H. Sherry, ed., *The Riverside Preachers* (New York: Pilgrim Press, 1978); James W. Cox, ed., *The Twentieth-Century Pulpit*, vol. 2 (Nashville: Abingdon Press, 1981).

16. Antoinette Brown, 1853, by the Congregational Church in Ohio, *www.ucc.org*.

17. David Albert Farmer and Edwina Hunter, eds., *Spinning a Sacred Yarn: Women Speak from the Pulpit* (New York: Pilgrim Press, 1982); David Albert Farmer and

are remarkable contributions to our homiletical history. The year 1989 saw the publication of a homiletic by, about, and for women written by homiletician Christine Smith and entitled *Weaving the Sermon: Preaching in a Feminist Perspective*. In this work, she reconstructs homiletical theory from a feminist perspective and believes that preaching should give a privileged place to women's stories and experiences. She uses biblical interpretation from a feminist liberation perspective to critique traditional homiletical theory that practices a hierarchy of power.[18]

The recorded history of African American preachers dates back to the Second Awakening when slaves became Christians and certain denominations recognized their preaching gifts. The number of African American preachers continued to increase, as did their reputation, occasionally outpacing their white clergy counterparts.[19] Two African American traditions emerged from their styles of preaching: "elite" being the literary or learned sermon and "folk" being the chanted or ecstatic sermon. Both of these traditions came together in the revered preacher Dr. Martin Luther King Jr. His style spoke to people of learning and at the same time had the rhythm, chant, climax, and hum by which the folk tradition is defined. King's famous "I Have a Dream" sermon is an excellent example of this combination. While there are many from which to choose, preacher and pastor at Riverside Church, New York, Rev. James Forbes's style of preaching follows in the folk tradition, while the preaching style of professor and minister at Harvard University Peter J. Gomes reflects the elite or literary tradition. Henry H. Mitchell authored *The Recovery of Preaching* in 1977, in which he upheld the traditional African American sermon with its

---

Edwina Hunter, eds., *And Blessed Is She: Sermons by Women* (San Francisco: Harper & Row, 1990); Barbara Brown Taylor, *Mixed Blessings* (Atlanta: Susan Hunter Publishing, 1986); Bettye Collier-Thomas, *Daughters of Thunder: Black Women Preachers and Their Sermons, 1850–1979* (San Francisco: Jossey-Bass, 1998).

18. Christine M. Smith, *Weaving the Sermon: Preaching in a Feminist Perspective* (Louisville: Westminster John Knox Press, 1989).

19. Edwards, *A History of Preaching*, 529–30.

storytelling form and reinforcement of oral traditions used by African Americans during slavery.[20]

Currently, *Pulpito* is one of the few books available that addresses the distinctive issues and characteristics of Latino preaching in mainline Protestant denominations. Authors Justo Gonzales and Pablo Jimenez discuss important historical, theoretical, and methodological issues in Hispanic homiletics, primarily within the United States. Their book includes ten sermons by various Latino or Hispanic voices.[21] Latino churches are among some of the fastest-growing churches within North America, and their preaching styles bring a relevant voice to white American theology and homiletics.

An Asian American perspective on homiletics authored by Eunjoo Mary Kim draws spiritual aspects from her Korean culture to create spiritual hermeneutics and a model for spiritual preaching.[22] This method recognizes an intuitive meditation like in Buddhism and Confucianism, as well as in the ancient Christian practice of *lectio divina*, as a form of biblical interpretation. Rather than use a traditional historical criticism or an imaginary approach, this hermeneutic centers on a spiritual practice with the biblical text that lends itself to new meaning — the exegesis for the sermon. The influence of Asian communication and rhetorical theories in this homiletic create a spiral-shaped sermon form. Kim's theology underpinning this homiletic rests on the presence of the Holy Spirit in the preacher and congregation as the sermon is given. The authority and power of the

---

20. James Forbes, *The Holy Spirit and Preaching* (Nashville: Abingdon Press, 1989), Peter J. Gomes, *Sermons: Biblical Wisdom for Daily Living* (New York: William Morrow, 1998); Henry H. Mitchell, *The Recovery of Preaching* (San Francisco: Harper & Row, 1977); see also Henry H. Mitchell, *Black Preaching: The Recovery of a Powerful Art* (Nashville: Abingdon Press, 1991).

21. Justo L. Gonzales and Catherine G. Gonzales, *Liberation Preaching: The Pulpit and the Oppressed* (Nashville: Abingdon Press, 1980), and *The Liberation Pulpit* (Nashville: Abingdon Press, 1994); Justo Gonzales and Pablo A. Jimenez, eds., *Pulpito: An Introduction to Hispanic Preaching* (Nashville: Abingdon Press, 2005).

22. Eunjoo Mary Kim, *Preaching the Presence of God: A Homiletic from an Asian American Perspective* (Valley Forge, PA: Judson Press, 1999).

sermon depend solely on God's Spirit and not on any human quality or position.[23]

Another unique recent homiletical resource is one for and about persons with disabilities. Author Kathy Black instructs preachers how people living with disabilities might hear and receive sermons when preachers are unaware of physical limitations some people live with daily. She studies the miracles performed through Jesus and the spiritual healing involved with an eye toward how they sound for those whose disability is not immediately or ever "healed" in the traditional sense. *A Healing Homiletic* brings into our awareness the large numbers of people living with disabilities in our faith communities and offers a new method of preaching about healing based on Scripture.[24]

God Comes Out therefore follows in this long line of homiletical resources from particular perspectives. In it, I construct a homiletical theory from a self-identified lesbian white minister's perspective. Speaking out of my experience limits what I can offer with regard to gay men, bisexual, and transgender preaching perspectives. Yet the coming out experience for the various sexual minorities is similar. Intentionally, I have kept the LGBT nomenclature throughout the book to remind us of their presence in our pulpits and in so doing to call forth their contributions to this homiletic. While this homiletic will not speak for all in the LGBT faith communities, it is my hope and prayer that it will speak for some and spark conversation and debate. I have included many other voices in the LGBT community who, once at the margins, are now finding themselves as leaders of congregations. The voices of those long silenced by society's view of their sexual orientation and gender identity bring a unique message of truth telling to churches. Ten sermons serve as illustrations for the LGBT homiletic as it develops from one chapter to the next. Each sermon was carefully selected for the voice it represents, the homiletical insights that can be gained, the LGBT theology, and its challenges to the local church.

---

23. Ibid., 69.

24. Kathleen Black, *A Healing Homiletic: Preaching and Disability* (Nashville: Abingdon Press, 1996).

This book may also break the silence in which closeted LGBT clergy live in which they do not have the opportunity to preach in a way that is true to their own being. The possibility of losing one's ordination or position is always lurking. This reality also shapes a homiletic that will take seriously the lives of LGBT clergy, including those who cannot speak out publicly. The homiletic will show that preaching with integrity from the center of one's being is part of God's coming out process too.

The Chapters Ahead

Coming out as a naming of oneself as a lesbian woman or a gay man, a bisexual or transgendered person is a profound experience and deserves theological attention and study. Chapter 2 focuses primarily on the coming out experience of lesbians and gay men. Coming out as a bisexual or transgendered person has different implications with which I am not as familiar and are thus better dealt with by persons with this experience. For the most part, this study serves as a foundation upon which to build future homiletical theories by those in the sexual minority community. While I do not have extensive knowledge of all sexual minorities — I have only one particular experience from which to write — what I offer is my contribution to the greater homiletical endeavor of proclaiming the gospel.

Coming out can be traumatic in itself; society often makes it harder either by their ignorance and misunderstanding or through fear of the other. For all the pain we endure as minorities, something must be noted. Writing about humanity, Irish poet Seamus Heaney comments poignantly that nothing can fully right those things done that harm and are wrong.[25] As his poem continues, not giving up hope, Heaney urges us to avoid revenge and believe in a place that is both attainable and miraculous — justice. The pain and misery of the human condition is acknowledged but not trivialized by an imagined future that

---

25. Seamus Heaney, "Voices from Lemnos," in *Opened Ground: Selected Poems, 1966–1996* (New York: Farrar, Straus and Giroux, 1998), 305–6.

holds new life breaking forth — "when hope and history rhyme" and justice prevails.

It is time for "hope" and "history" to rhyme once again. To proceed toward hope we must endeavor to include and honor the coming out experience. Two sermons are therefore included in each chapter and then analyzed with respect to the LGBT homiletic. They illustrate the concepts in the given chapter.

Most if not all Christian sermons begin with the Bible, and LGBT preachers are no different in that respect. Yet what will become apparent as the coming out process is applied to biblical exegesis is the different interpretations that result from viewing the Bible through the eyes of sexual minorities. Chapter 3 therefore considers the ways LGBT clergy use the Bible in their sermon preparation and preaching. Two sermons offered here are by lesbian preachers, one closeted and one out. Their sermons take everyday items like weeds and lost coins and weave them into instructive theological lessons. Interestingly, though, the out preacher does not mention LGBT persons in the sermon and the closeted preacher does. What does this indicate about identity in regard to an LGBT homiletic?

In chapter 4, theology comes out with critical thinking by LGBT people about the presence of God in the LGBT community and the wider church. Already, many books by lesbian, gay, bisexual, and transgender people are on the shelves of our libraries and bookstores.[26] But how do we sift through these new theologies? Is there one that would best serve our homiletic? In the vein of liberation theology, LGBT theology flows into queer theology as it intersects with queer academic theory. Three theological concepts are reviewed: creation, incarnation, and resurrection. Each concept shares the theme of body, which is important for LGBT persons. The two sermons included in

---

26. Among those is Gary David Comstock, *A Whosoever Church: Welcoming Lesbians and Gay Men into African American Congregations* (Louisville: Westminster John Knox Press, 2001); Debra Kolodny, ed., *Blessed Bi Spirit* (New York: Continuum, 2000); and Justin Tanis, *Trans-gendered: Theology, Ministry, and Communities of Faith* (Cleveland: Pilgrim Press, 2003).

this chapter offer a then-closeted gay man's view of incarnation and an out lesbian woman's view of resurrection. What is the impact of a sermon given by a closeted gay man versus an openly lesbian woman? What are the implications for developing an LGBT homiletic?

Chapter 5 is central to the work at hand: preaching. Preaching comes out of seclusion in the heterosexual world through an examination of communication theories and historical homiletical methods. The theory of "truth through personality" is in reference to what I call "whole body preaching." Speaking truth through our personality — including body, spirit, mind, and soul — communicates something of which we are not always conscious when preaching. These methodologies along with sermons help to identify four tasks of an LGBT homiletic. These tasks are based upon Buber's I-Thou model of relationships. The "I" in this case is the preacher and his or her relationship to four areas: Bible/theology, Thou/the other, us/justice, and spirit/intimacy. These tasks provide a beginning point for conversation about LGBT preaching. In this chapter, the sermons are by female clergy — one an out lesbian and the other a straight preacher. Each suggests a possible way preaching comes out on behalf of God and on behalf of LGBT people.

In chapter 6, God comes out through several approaches. Realizing that there is not one central idea of how the coming out of God would look or sound or be, I gather possibilities from several sources and consider the images of God as a lesbian, gay man, bisexual, or transgendered being and the impact of such a God-image within the Christian community. The two sermons are by out lesbian and gay clergypersons whose preaching is fully integrated in their lives, without worry about their positions, their listeners, their God. For them, God is fully out to their theological and creative energies that draw people into new images of this God through the eyes and lives of sexual minorities.

Finally, chapter 7 is an epilogue that includes findings from other preachers and a summary of the sermons included here. Ideally, having eliminated the "problem" or the "issue," we arrive at the world we envision that does not draw barriers around the Communion table but instead is so invested in the love of God and neighbor that Communion is served by our fabulously Queer God. Is it possible for God to come out through the preaching voices of those whose lives can honestly reflect and reveal the vivid ways God's diversity in human life is lived? The goal of all preaching is to bring God out of our spiritual closets; the LGBT homiletic does just this with a celebration of sexuality and clarity about the love of God in us. This encounter of God in preaching by LGBT and straight allies brings more truth and light to our lives — the continuing revelation of God in human history. Our sermons are the sound of hope and history rhyming.

Chapter 2

Coming Out

Coming out is a personal epiphany, a revelation, as Star Trek's Captain Hikaru Sulu can testify. His announcement in 2005 that he is gay and has a partner of eighteen years made the headlines. When asked if others knew he was "out," he offered this response to what "coming out" looks like:

> The word "out" seems to suggest opening a door and walking through a portal and suddenly the world changes. It's really not like that. I use the metaphor of a long, narrow corridor which is dark at first, then there are little glimmers of light coming in, then it starts to widen, and then there's a window opening. And you peek out, and you see some possibilities. And then there are doors ajar, and you might step out briefly and then come back in. So, it is a long process. It's not as the word "out" suggests — a sudden decision and you step into another world.[1]

"Coming out" is a term used to acknowledge that someone has self-identified as a lesbian, gay, bisexual, or transgendered person, a different status from the majority of people. Coming out is a process, not a one-time event. It may take years for someone to even come out to themselves let alone to begin to tell those closest to them. While it can be used in a variety of ways, the term "coming out" primarily refers to sexual or gender orientation.

Coming out almost always involves a reaction by others who need to adjust to this change in the emerging self. Some of those reactions

---

1. George Takei, interview in *Equality, Human Rights Campaign* (Winter 2006): 16.

can be supportive; others are very plainly not. Either way, coming out usually involves an acceptance of self as a sexual minority and an awareness that oppression exists for those who are not heterosexual.

A colleague of mine, who had just come out as a gay man to himself, his family, and the congregation he was serving, went on a personal retreat to Christ in the Desert Monastery, Abiquiu, New Mexico. When he returned, he shared this story with me about wrestling with God in the desert: each evening after dinner and matins at the monastery, he went outside to sit and watch the night come. As he sat there, watching the sky turn from bright blue to orange and pink, then to a darker color, he saw the stars come out. He thought about his own coming out and how painful the whole process had been of telling his wife, his kids, his family-of-origin, his staff, the pastor relations committee, the council, and finally the congregation. As he sobbed with grief over his losses, the stars began to appear in the night sky. The darker it became, the more stars became visible. In that part of the country, where there are few commercial lights, one can see a tremendous number of stars. For him, the stars coming out — coming into view in the night sky — were a metaphorical reminder that they have to come out every night too. The stars are there all day long, but we do not see them until the sun disappears in the western horizon. "Coming out" is a process that goes on as long as we are alive; at the same time as it is life giving, coming out can also feel as if the world is ending, and darkness is all around. The stars became a powerful symbol for my colleague as he found strength in his coming out journey.[2]

Coming out almost always involves loss, both personal — self-image, family, and friends — and political — basic rights like the option of getting married, health care being extended to one's partner, or legal status as a couple.

---

2. The Reverend Dr. Scott Landis, UCC, interview by author, April 2002, Denver, Colorado.

Carter Heyward is an Episcopal priest who self-disclosed as a lesbian
after her ordination and has retained her standing. Ordained in 1974,
prior to that denomination's agreement to ordain women as priests,
Heyward was one of the "irregular eleven" women who were ordained
two years prior to the vote. She came out as a lesbian two years later
and has continued to be an advocate for LGBT people and our allies.
As a professor of theology at Episcopal Divinity School, Heyward has
written and spoken frequently about sexuality and theology. Regarding
the coming out process, she writes:

> [C]oming out is a relational process associated with lesbians'
> and gay men's public affirmation of ourselves in relation to one
> another. Coming out of the closet in which our relational lives
> are kept from public view and, usually, condemnation, we move
> into a shared power. By this power, in this power, and with this
> power, we find ourselves-in-relation, breaking out of isolation
> imposed by silence and invisibility.[3]

While for some lesbian and gay men, the choice to come out is purely
for personal reasons and not political, being out nevertheless increases
the visibility of lesbians and gays who in turn form a subculture and
community. One may not be coming out in order to connect with the
larger community or to stand in resistance to the oppression of lesbian,
gay, bisexual, or transgender people, yet it does have that effect. When
a homosexual chooses to come out, she or he makes visible what was
not visible — like stars becoming visible at nighttime. In this way,
while choosing to come out is a personal process, it has the effect
of increasing the visibility of all LGBT persons in society. Heyward's
point that by coming out we can find ourselves in relation to another
is important for the connections we make with other oppressions in
our society and with the basic fear that keeps us alienated from one
another. Sexual orientation is like any other culturally constructed

---

3. Carter Heyward, *Touching Our Strength: The Erotic as Power and the Love of
God* (San Francisco: Harper & Row Publishers, 1989), 21.

social system such as race, gender identity, economic power, ethnicity, or disability that keeps us from being in human connection. Thus, it is a profoundly theological issue, because being in human connection brings us into our awareness of the Divine.

Staying In

It is a personal matter for each gay person to decide whether they want to come out, since there are situations where disclosing the truth could place one in harm's way. One has the constant fear of being rejected by others; the losses that will occur are real, and no one can make that decision for someone else. If there were truly no oppression toward gay or lesbian persons, then probably this decision would not be so monumental. And it is precisely because of such oppression that truth telling about one's sexual orientation is often discouraged; lying is often considered the wiser option when it comes to a job or promotion. In reality, many mainline denominations have policies against the ordination of gay and lesbian persons which can force a silence upon candidates for ordination. If candidates tell the truth, they will be denied ordination. Lying about whom one loves is not healthy, as it reflects negatively on who we are as creations of God and who God is as Creator. Nancy Wilson, a Metropolitan Community Church pastor and now president of that denomination, says, "After all the fear, lying, and hiding, telling the truth is positively sacramental. It is a rite of purification."[4] For me, to keep silent about my sexual orientation was to agree with my oppressors that it is a bad or immoral practice, rather than a life-giving one. So I believe that coming out is a theological statement about where and who God is in the world. All this said, it is still important to realize that coming out can and has led to rejection, loss of job, violence, and even death. Some people are not in positions where coming out is life-giving. The

---

4. Nancy Wilson, *Our Tribe: Queer Folk, God, Jesus, and the Bible* (San Francisco: HarperSanFrancisco, 1995), 43.

decision to remain closeted demands respect and acknowledgment as well.

Christian and LGBT

To some Christians, suggesting that God created a person as gay just as God created another as left-handed is a radical statement. More radical still to some is the consequent extrapolation that if, as gay or bisexual or transgender, we are created in the image of God, then an aspect of God is homosexual or bisexual or transgender too. Is that what those who oppose homosexual clergy and members fear — that God will come out as LGBT?

God comes out through the voices of lesbian and gay church members and out clergy, but the path to reclaim self-acceptance and membership in the Christian church is long and winding. For many LGBT people, being active in the Christian community is not an inviting prospect due to outspoken Christian leaders who openly oppose and vilify homosexuals. Since there are not many messages affirming homosexuality in our culture, nor in the church, growing up in a predominantly heterosexual world for those who are not heterosexual is complicated. People who do not experience their same-sex orientation mirrored back to them in some healthy and reasonable way typically suffer from a loss of self. If we were to consider what rules should be binding in society and construct a just society that does not discriminate on the basis of race, class, gender, sexual orientation, age, and so forth, then we might see another side to the argument. A case study of ethics puts it this way, "For example, if we did not know whether we would be male or female, straight or gay, black or white, migrant worker or CEO of a major corporation, we might be forced to stretch our imaginations when seeking to structure a just society."[5] This being the case, would we not want a society in

---

5. Robert L. Stivers et al., eds., *Christian Ethics: A Case Method Approach* (Maryknoll, NY: Orbis Books, 2000), 256.

which we are treated with dignity and respect regardless of our human condition?

Gay and lesbian persons live in a culture pervaded with messages that homosexuality is wrong, sick, bad, criminal, and irreligious. In our particular U.S. culture, these messages stem mostly from Christianity. In church school, camp, and worship, many of us grew up singing, "Jesus loves me, this I know, for the Bible tells me so ... ," and "Just as I am without one plea ... " Yet the authority of those words evaporated when we came out, and instead of being told Jesus loves us we are told we're an abomination in the sight of God.

While we know virtually nothing about the young man who sought out Professor Buber, we do know that it was because he did not find in the conversation with Buber the human connection he so desperately sought at that moment that he ended up killing himself. It is this human connection, this ultimate acceptance of self, as Paul Tillich called it, for which we all yearn. In some situations, we find humans willing to mirror this acceptance back to us by accepting us until we can accept ourselves. In other situations when no one is present, a person struggling to live while so unaccepted by others may end her life in suicide. Indeed, many teenage suicide studies note that sexual orientation is one of the highest reasons for suicide attempts. Whether they are lesbian, gay, or questioning their sexuality, teenagers' fear of rejection can be so overwhelming that there seem to be no alternatives other than suicide. This is an indication of how strongly our society reinforces heterosexuality. That Christianity in general denounces homosexuality so severely leads some extremists to believe that it is best to do away with anyone at all outside the norm of Christianity, regardless of their essential humanity. Unbridled hatred thus finds support in Christianity and can result in death through violence toward a gay person.

In his book *The Good Book: Reading the Bible with Mind and Heart*, Rev. Peter J. Gomes includes a chapter on homosexuality and the Bible. In it, he recounts the story of the intentional killing of a young gay man and addresses subsequent research on the case:

In preparing for her novel *The Drowning of Stephen Jones,* based on the true story of a young gay man tossed from a bridge to his death by a group of young gay-bashers, author Bette Greene interviewed more than four hundred young men in jail for various forms of gay-bashing. Few of the men, she noted, showed any remorse for their crimes. Few saw anything morally wrong with their crimes, and more than a few of them told her that they were justified in their opinions and in their actions by the religious traditions from which they came. Homosexuality was wrong, and against the Bible. One of those interviewed told her that the pastor of his church had said that homosexuals represented Satan and the Devil. The implication of his logic was clear: Who could possibly do wrong in destroying Satan and all of his works? The legitimization of violence against homosexuals and Jews and women and blacks, as we have seen, comes from the view that the Bible stigmatizes these people thereby making them fair game. If the Bible expresses such a prejudice, then it certainly cannot be wrong to act on that prejudice. This, of course, is the argument every anti-Semite and racist has used with demonstrably devastating consequences, as our social history all too vividly shows.[6]

While this may be an extreme example of a Christian church environment, it can nonetheless be true that more genuine acceptance and kindness toward LGBT persons can be found among those not raised within the Christian church.

There are numerous stories to tell of women and men who know themselves to be homosexual and feel rejection by their particular church. One person's story does not represent all, but it does offer a glimpse of what many, including myself, have struggled through to come out within the Christian tradition. Stories such as the one that follows can be found in families, churches, and books that have

---

6. Peter J. Gomes, *The Good Book: Reading the Bible with Mind and Heart* (New York: Avon Books, 1996), 146.

recorded these experiences to let others know how it feels to be a threatened minority.

> Over a number of years, I had been engaged in a mortal internal struggle, an ongoing inner battle that kept me anxious, depressed and at times, practically immobilized. I knew what I felt inside, but I had been told by culture and church that these feelings were wrong and unacceptable. Was I thus defective? An aberration or abomination? Or was I like everybody else, an expression of God's wondrous diversity in creation?[7]

It is because our society, especially the church, upholds heterosexuality and "one man–one woman" as the definition of family that we live in a web of heterosexism that inhibits our efforts toward inclusion and genuine openness. Most gay men and lesbians at some time in their lives have been fearful that if their sexual orientation were to become known, they would be the object of harassment, violence, or discrimination at work, in school, in their churches, in the emergency room, in their families of origin, in their neighborhood and communities. To be thus treated in any one of these areas would be struggle enough; collectively they form a complex web of oppression that for lesbians and gay men enforces either invisibility or the need to risk it all by coming out. To argue that "coming out" is a theological category of its own requires a closer examination of homophobia and heterosexism.

Homophobia

The word "homophobia" was originally coined in 1972 by psychotherapist Dr. George Weinberg and was defined as "the dread of being

---

7. Sylvia Thorson-Smith, *Reconciling the Broken Silence* (Louisville: Christian Education Program Area of the Congregational Ministry Division of the PC[USA], 1992), 59.

in close quarters with a homosexual — and in the case of homosexuals themselves, self-loathing."[8] Homophobia, as understood in its
common usage, is an irrational fear or hatred of homosexual people.
It includes the fear of others who are homosexual, the fear of being
homosexual oneself, and the fear of any behavior in oneself that might
be interpreted as homosexual. It is a form of prejudice and discrimination. A United Church of Christ minister and author, Leanne Tigert,
amplifies the definition, "Homophobia is a form and manifestation of
prejudice or prejudgment. It is a combination of beliefs, attitudes, and
opinions that one has preformed, based on myths, assumptions, and
stereotypes."[9]

In today's usage, homophobia is a derogatory term used when
referencing another person's intolerance toward gay and lesbian individuals. As a minister in four different churches, I have observed
how nonhomosexual people will go to great lengths to avoid a homophobic perception of themselves by others. Congregants let me know
that they do not hate and are not afraid of gay people. Though this
was helpful to balance out those in the congregation who made their
hostility known — for example, by openly stating that they do not
want the homosexual minister to call on them, or preside at their funeral or wedding — my congregants' candor still was not fully honest
because everyone, even gay people, carries homophobia within them.
We cannot help it, just as we cannot claim we are not racist in a privileged white society. What begins to make a difference is what we do
with that privilege.

For example, at a church committee meeting, an out lesbian member identified her own homophobia in a public discourse and people
were stunned. Other members did not perceive that homosexual
people suffer from homophobia. Evidently there is a general misunderstanding and denial about homophobia in churches, even those who

---

8. George Weinberg, *Society and the Healthy Homosexual* (New York: St. Martin's
Press, 1974), 4.

9. Leanne Tigert, *Coming Out through Fire* (Cleveland: Pilgrim Press, 1999), 11.

have stated that they are open and affirming or welcoming. Catholic feminist theologian Mary Hunt states, "Homophobia is a powerful tool in the church and society where people are too frightened to talk about and listen to the variety of ways people can love. Homophobia keeps many of us from learning about the unknown, and from facing the unacceptable."[10]

Heterosexism

Given the confusions, discomforts, and limitations of the terminology of homophobia, a new framework in the continuing discourse is needed. The term "heterosexism" helps to reframe oppression of homosexuality in a new way, thus giving preachers, scholars, and theologians more possibility for formulating a constructive contribution. Heterosexism is related to homophobia and is defined as the underlying cultural assumption that everyone is, and should be, heterosexual.

Episcopal priest and feminist lesbian theologian Carter Heyward describes heterosexism as "the system by which heterosexuality is assumed to be the only acceptable and viable life option.... Because this norm is so pervasive, heterosexism is difficult to detect.... It forces lesbians, gays, and bisexuals to struggle constantly against their own invisibility. Heterosexism is an inherent form of political, social and legal injustice."[11] Heyward goes on to explain, "Heterosexism is the logical extension of sexism and serves the same purpose of controlling women's bodies and lives through this structuring of alienated power."[12] Stated this way, the concern about inclusion of homosexuals becomes more obvious and crucial than simply a fear of the other (homophobia); it is in fact both oppressive and unjust.

---

10. Mary Hunt, "Same-Sex Love in American Religion," Iliff School of Theology lecture, July 2002, Denver, Colorado (permission granted in e-mail).

11. Heyward, *Touching Our Strength,* 50.

12. Ibid., 51.

Authors Patricia Beattie Jung and Ralph Smith in their textbook *Heterosexism* further sharpen the definition of heterosexism to be "a reasoned system of bias regarding sexual orientation. It denotes prejudice against bisexual and, especially, homosexual people. By describing it as a reasoned system of prejudice we do not mean to imply that it is rationally defensible. . . . It is rooted in a largely cognitive constellation of beliefs about human sexuality."[13] Heterosexism is about privilege and special provisions that come with being a member of the dominant sexual orientation group. Some examples: as a heterosexual, a person can legally marry their loved one, receive numerous financial benefits, file joint income tax returns, have the right to make important decisions when a spouse is incapacitated, and pass on property to the other upon death. Furthermore, heterosexuals receive cultural approval and support for their relationships; they can talk about and engage in conversation at work regarding their spouses without having to worry about whether people will give disapproving stares, or worse, discriminate against them.

It is a simple matter of justice. Yet when one congregation I served went through the two-year process toward becoming an "Open and Affirming" church, the inclusion of homosexuals (much less bisexual or transgender people) was not examined as a justice matter at all. Instead, the matter was determined by whether church members perceived homosexuality to be acceptable or sinful. Those members who perceived homosexuality to be outside of the Christian realm of correct behavior did not support the ONA vote. If they perceived it to be "acceptable," then they would vote for ONA; if they had a family member who was gay or knew someone, they would support the vote. Either way it was not a matter of justice, but a matter of how one felt toward the person who was gay or lesbian. And how one felt typically was directly dependent on whether one had a close connection to a gay or lesbian person.

---

13. Patricia Beattie Jung and Ralph F. Smith, *Heterosexism: An Ethical Challenge* (New York: State University of New York Press, 1993), 13.

Such feelings were typically also expressed quite crassly in people's language. Those members who felt negative toward the ONA vote or discussion about lesbians and gays usually referred to a homosexual person as "it," whereas those members who were supportive of ONA would say "person" or "lesbian" or "gay" rather than always referring elusively and pejoratively to "it" or the "issue."

Doing Justice

Such language and such attitudes echo Buber's theology of "I-It" and "I-Thou." Instead of objectifying the person, gay or straight, a relationship invites the persons into being present with one another. From a justice perspective, affirmation toward lesbian and gay people would look like a commitment to the biblical understanding of justice as exhibited in the Hebrew Scriptures and the Gospels, rather than what one perceives to be within the norm. Repeatedly in the biblical story, God sent prophets to remind Israel that they are to welcome the stranger, look after their neighbor, care for the widows, walk humbly, do justice, and love kindness. The prophet Amos's words are rather biting about what God really desires, which is justice:

> I hate, I despise your festivals, and I take no delight in your solemn assemblies. Even though you offer me your burnt offerings and grain offerings, I will not accept them. . . . But let justice roll down like waters, and righteousness like an ever flowing stream. (Amos 5:21–22, 24)

The description of heterosexism used by Heyward spells out justice issues regarding homosexuals in the life of the church, as well as society. She argues that the law does not protect homosexuals and that discrimination is an ongoing experience. That LGBT people are relegated to a second-class citizenship sends a message that it is acceptable to ostracize, hurt, maim, and kill. This alone should be sufficient reason for Christians to wrestle with homosexuality from a theological perspective. One begins doing this by listening to the lives of lesbian and gay people rather than making sweeping judgments. To that end, having more out lesbian and gay preachers is a significant beginning in hearing the gospel through the lives of those who have been marginalized and excluded from leadership within the Christian church. For throughout the biblical story, God is on the side of the oppressed, the powerless, the widows, the orphans, and the marginalized. While there are only a few biblical texts that deal with sexual behavior, and one specifically about male-to-male and female-to-female sexual behavior, the overarching story is about a God who is constantly reaching out to the people and inviting them to join the tribe. As a counterpoint to those who appeal to the Bible for support of their condemnation of certain sexual behaviors, author Bruce Hilton reminds us of other stipulations within the biblical text that we tend to ignore:

> We forget that the Bible's power is in its great themes relevant to every age — not specific commands designed for a time and situation centuries ago. The priestly rules in Leviticus, which forbade the crossbreeding of cattle, or the blending of cotton and wool in a robe, were set down at a time when the Israelites' identity as a separate people was threatened — during or just after exile.[14]

Jesus never once mentioned homosexuality, but he talked often about money, divorce, and the poor. Those who refer to the Bible to denounce homosexuality would do well to follow Jesus in paying more attention to those matters instead.

The Churches' Coming Out Process

In 1986 at a National Gathering of the United Church of Christ Coalition for Lesbian and Gay Concerns, Gary Comstock described what was happening as more and more lesbians and gay men chose to live open lives:

---

14. Bruce Hilton, *Can Homophobia Be Cured?* (Nashville: Abingdon Press, 1992), 60–61.

While it may not have been our intention, I think we have to face squarely that our very lives, when lived openly and fully, fundamentally threaten the social order [I would add the ecclesiastical order as well]. When we begin to make decisions for ourselves, instead of letting others tell us how we should live, we challenge those who have power at the expense of the disempowered and marginalized.[15]

This statement spoken over twenty years ago is still true as we witness old laws being repealed and new ones like hate crime legislation coming into effect. The old sodomy laws were repealed in Texas by the U.S. Supreme Court on June 26, 2003, and the Massachusetts State Supreme Court added an amendment to legalize gay marriage on May 17, 2004. An increasing number of same-sex marriages are taking place without laws in effect. In addition, American couples can travel to Canada to be legally married in that country. In many ways, social advances for the LGBT community are coming rapidly — while churches continue to debate whether homosexuality is a sin. Chances are the church will soon find itself overtaken and outmoded. Gay author and Englishman Quentin Crisp offered an uncanny truth in his 1968 autobiography, *The Naked Civil Servant:*

In an expanding universe, time is on the side of the outcast. Those who once inhabited the suburbs of human contempt find that without changing their address they eventually live in the metropolis.[16]

While Crisp's quotation speaks honestly and offers hope, it is also a reflection of more people coming out publicly. It takes time to live into this acceptance of self as other than heterosexual. Many times it seems easier to be invisible like the stars in my colleague's desert story.

---

15. Gary David Comstock, "Aliens in a Promised Land?" Keynote Address for the 1986 National Gathering of the United Church of Christ's Coalition for Lesbian and Gay Concerns.

16. Quentin Crisp, *The Naked Civil Servant* (London: Jonathan Cape, 1968; New York: Penguin Books, 1997), 2.

Some clergy do choose to remain silent about their orientation. In some cases, it is necessary to do so — or risk losing their ordination, as many clergy have. Those who do come out while in ministry can create opportunities for engagement about sexuality. The word "crisis" also means opportunity. This happened recently in the United Methodist Church, when the Reverend Karen Dammann revealed herself as a lesbian woman with a partner and a child. A church trial with thirteen pastors as jury acquitted her of the charge of violating church doctrine as "a self-avowed, practicing homosexual."[17] Fortunately, when my colleague came out he did not face a formal denominational charge of violating church doctrine. He faced a different sort of church trial that forced the congregation to look at its heterosexual privilege.

&

What follows are two sermons that in different ways address the personal nature of coming out. The first is a personal coming out story by an out gay clergyman that illustrates the struggle to identify himself within the Christian church and remain true to his self-knowledge as a gay man.

The second is by a straight, married clergyman whose sermon comes out in support of lesbian and gay people — though the Christian church has often persecuted them. Both sermons were preached on or around "National Coming Out Day" (October 10), but for strikingly difference reasons — one a pastor's story at an ONA UCC church, the other at the funeral of Matthew Shepard. The first sermon, by Reverend Dan Geslin, a pastor of Sixth Avenue United Church of Christ in Denver, Colorado, was preached October 9, 2005. Before coming to that position he served as founding pastor of Spirit of the Lakes UCC in Minneapolis and Liberty UCC in Cleveland. He also worked as a chaplain in a hospital in San Francisco during the height of the AIDS crisis.

---

17. Shannon Dininny, "Methodists Praise, Assail Acquittal of Lesbian Pastor," *Denver Post,* March 22, 2004, section A, 2.

Sermon:
"A COMING OUT STORY"
by Dan Geslin

Texts: Exodus 3:14; John 3:1–6; Ephesians 3:16–20

When I was twenty-something, I experienced God's call to the ministry of Word and Sacrament. That may sound grand and spiritual, but when I say "call" I do not mean that I was struck by a bolt of lightning in any magical sense, but rather "call" as the story of my life. In fact, when people ask me how I came to be a pastor, I never know if I should begin with the story of starting the first gay-lesbian church in the UCC, or the story of going to seminary, or the story of my parents baptizing me Daniel . . . as in the lions' den.

When I experienced God's call in my twenties, I was just out of college, teaching school in the suburbs during the week and going out (as opposed to coming out) to inner-city gay bars in Minneapolis on the weekends. In my memory it is always winter and I remember my "hidden inner self" on Friday nights, parking in the dark warehouse district, walking its dim-lit streets, and then being hit by the neon lights of Hennepin Avenue. I'd walk fast through the dirty downtown, my eyes lowered, past pornographic book stores, straight strip joints, and prostitutes in doorways in black leather miniskirts, stiletto heels, and bare legs in the raw cold of the night. I had a big brown Dr. Zhivago coat with a big collar I'd pull up around my face, because I was afraid. My biggest fear in life was that someone who I knew would see me go into a gay bar, and then they would know . . . who I am.

Yet it was in my fear that I first heard God calling me to faith. But when I say that I heard God's call, I do not mean that the sky split open and I saw an enlightening vision of safety, security, and peace. On the contrary, my call was a painful struggle between my gigantic fear and a tiny vision of faith that was beginning to germinate inside me. I remember sitting alone in my one-bedroom apartment reading

The Advocate from cover to cover and slowly coming to believe that, if I could just get to San Francisco, I would be born again into a New Life. That little fantasy of hope became my call.

But the paradox of my call was that the more hope I had, the more pain I felt. Because God would not leave me in peace. God kept bugging me. At my most vulnerable moments, God's voice inside me would call out to me: "Dan, what are you doing here? — Dan, why are you hiding like this? — Dan, where is your self-respect?" I was angry at God for confronting and shaming and pushing me. Didn't God understand that I was just a poor, oppressed victim? — that there was nothing I could do about myself? If there was a God — which I seriously doubted — a God who loved me, then God should stop shaming me and just help me hide. That was what I really needed: I needed to feel safe and secure and well hidden. But instead, God kept confronting my fear with a call to faith.

So things were hard for me inside myself, because I was haunted by my baptism, by the way I had been brought up — "planted in love and rooted in love" — in the church of my childhood. I could remember that, before I had realized who I am, I had known the spiritual gifts of friendship and trust and integrity, had felt free and open about myself. But now my "secret" paralyzed my spirit and cut me off from all those spiritual things like love, inner peace, and integrity. (In the bar scene I only met people pretending to be free by getting high.) And of course, I had not gone to church for years because it was always stupid and boring and usually oppressive. But I thought, "Maybe, just maybe, if I go to seminary, I can find an intelligent approach to Christianity." So I applied to the Lutheran seminary in Berkeley . . . across the Bay Bridge from San Francisco.

I knew the safe thing to do was to stay put. I had the security of a good job, and I remember thinking that, even though I could not be honest at my job, now was the time to buy a house and buy a car and buy a stereo — I could have everything — I just could not have . . . who I am. But finally the scale of fear and faith tipped; my fear of the unknown was outweighed by my faith in the unknown.

Notice: I am not saying I had faith in the church or faith in the catechism answers or faith in the Bible. I am not talking about "Christianity." I am talking about my *life*.

So in Jesus' words, I gave up my life in order to find it. I quit my job, sold everything I had, and took the Greyhound bus to Berkeley.

Going to seminary was as much about being gay as it was about being "spiritual." What I would learn in seminary is that, for me, being gay and being spiritual are the same thing, because that is...who I am. God was calling me by name. In seminary I learned God's name: YHWH — "I AM WHO I AM" — and learning that I am created in I AM's image. God was calling me to become...who I am!

Someone here may be thinking, "Why is he talking about gay stuff in the pulpit instead of God?" Or, "I am not gay, so what does this have to do with me?" What I am trying to tell you is that God is not calling you to become someone else, like the fundamentalists say. God is calling you to become...who you are. I am trying to tell you that the text is not the Bible. The text is your own life. God's call is not magic from on high; it is the story of your life. This sermon is my testament. And I study the lives in the Old and New Testaments to learn how to interpret my own life. What we are talking about is life. How many of you really think that when Jesus told Nicodemus that he had to be "born again," he was telling him he had to join Focus on the Family? No, Jesus was talking about something psychological — psycho/spiritual — a lens through which we see life. God calling me to go to seminary and to San Francisco was the call to find myself, as a minister and as a gay man.

To follow that call was not the smart thing to do...it was illogical. But I was following my heart, following God's word of promise toward some sort of sacramental connection with life, with God, with self. That sacramental connection happened almost immediately as school started. I joined a Monday night rap group at Berkeley's Lesbian and Gay Community Center — something I never dared to do in Minneapolis for fear I would run into someone I knew and then they would know...who I am.

As the rap group began, I heard a handsome voice, deep, like the voice of a cello, speaking with intelligence. My eyes followed the sound of his voice around the circle until I saw a black-haired muscular man, movie-star handsome in cowboy boots, blue jeans, and a brown flannel shirt. I would later learn that [man] was Rafael ("Raf"), a third-generation Portuguese-Californian who worked as a gay rights lobbyist in Sacramento and was well connected with the politicians and leaders of the lesbian and gay community in San Francisco.

During the coffee hour that followed our rap group, Raf introduced himself to me and said that he lived in Napa Valley, where all the vineyards are. I told him I had just moved here from Minneapolis and was homesick for the colors of autumn — October is still summer in California.

The following Monday night, Raf again approached me during the coffee hour. He handed me one of those dark brown accordion legal pouches. When I opened it up, it was full of orange, yellow, and purple grape leaves. Raf had walked out into the vineyards and picked them just for me. Was I swept off my feet?

Our love was my first experience of trust in a way that I had never known before. It was sacramental in that I was able to transfer our relational trust into my relationship with God, in the same way that we transfer being fed in communion to the way God feeds us in community. Faith is not security; faith is insecurity. Faith is not knowing; faith is trusting. Faith frees us to be open and vulnerable and explore the unknown. And if we make mistakes, or we get hurt or we meet someone else who has made mistakes, faith is about forgiveness and grace and offering ourselves and each other New Life. In fact, to this day, when a fundamentalist asks me if I have been born again, I say, "Yes, about 10:00 p.m. on October 27, which is when Raf and I first made love."

Because that was the moment of conversion in my life; that was the moment when I knew that being gay is not about "sex," it is about love. That was the moment when I finally understood that God was not calling me to become someone different, God was calling me to become . . . who I am. That was the moment when I finally trusted that God has goodness in store for me, even when I cannot see it ahead of time, if only I could come out as a person of faith. That revelation was a "born again" experience.

When Jesus told Nicodemus that he needed to be born again of the Spirit in order to find the Community of God, he was using our physical birth as a poetic image to try to call us to a psychological birth in the image of the God whose name is I AM WHO I AM. We get so used to hearing the Bible stories that we forget how shocking and offensive the gospel really is at first hearing. The so-called good news first strikes us as bad news because it confronts us with a vision of inclusivity that demands that we change by accepting both ourselves and each other as we are.

For example, no sooner had I settled into my second year of seminary, feeling at home in that seminary community and having fun learning all this book knowledge about integrating my faith and life, than that very same gospel, that very same good news turned on me again and started bugging me with a call to put my faith into practice and come out to my bishop back in Minnesota, even though that meant I would be barred from ordination in the Lutheran Church. But God kept bugging me with a new question: Was my call to the security of the institution? Or was my call to Jesus' vision of inclusive community and to the integrity of who God created me to be?

That December, Raf and I went to a Christmas party in San Francisco, and many community leaders were there. It was four months before Harvey Milk was assassinated and four months before I had to go back to Minnesota for my matriculation interview with my bishop. I talked with Harvey about losing my career in ministry if I came out, yet wanting to be true to my faith. Harvey was Jewish, and he responded to my fear by teasing me about my name. "Do you know how the story of Daniel in the lions' den ends?" he asked. "Sure," I replied. "Well," Harvey smiled, "Daniel didn't."

Do you see the relation between the text of the Bible and the text of your life? I am not saved/liberated/made whole by believing that Daniel kept his faith in the lions' den. I am saved by keeping my own faith in my own lions' den. Harvey was confronting me with the vision of my own faith, and I knew he was right. He was lifting up the prophetic Hebrew vision of the Community of God. The Bible is not a science book; it is a sacrament, through which we share a communal vision.

One last time I want to say — this is not about Christianity, this is about life. Our baptismal call to be born again in the image of the God named I AM WHO I AM is a call to leave here today and live this vision out in our own lives. My sacramental love with Raf blessed me with the integrity to fulfill my prophetic call and come out to my bishop. That meant my faith required me to lose my life in order to save it, again. Twenty years ago God was promising me a future I could not see. When I lost my life in the Lutheran Church, I had no way of knowing that the UCC and all you loving people would be here offering me new life. When I took the step of coming out, I could not "see" my future. I could only act on the vision of my faith — a vision of becoming myself through faith. What makes us a church is being born again as a congregation that shares Jesus' vision that, one day, all people will embrace the faith that we are each created in the image of God and therefore all have the right to say: I AM WHO I AM. AMEN.

Analysis

The preacher's concept of one's life as the text rather than only the Bible as text helps to offset a primary weapon used against LGBT people — namely, the Bible. Rev. Geslin does not try to defend his life using the Bible, but instead he understands his life as the central text through which God calls him, and also us. His honesty about how God confronts, challenges, and corrals him helps the hearer know that responding to God's call is not always easy or acceptable. God calls him to grow up into his full identity as a gay man and to take responsibility for his call and life. In doing this, Rev. Geslin is clear that he loses his life at least two times in this story, which illustrates his biblical interpretation of John's Gospel about being born again, losing your life to find it, and replacing faith with fear. It is very touching and daring that he points to his sexual encounter as the place and time when he was born again. How rare it is for a sermon to speak so forthrightly about the experience of intimacy with another, despite how common such intimacy is among us. Furthermore, in his coming out narrative, Rev. Geslin offers an important truth that could be missed: "it is about love, not sex," he insists. So often the debate about homosexuals within the Christian church gets boiled down to sex. In this way, the debate has objectified sex at the same time it has objectified the person into an issue. Though our love for another leads us to express it in a physical or sexual way, that is not the only way we can express our love.

❧

The second sermon was given at a memorial service for slain student Matthew Shepard on October 10, 1998. Shepard, a gay man, was brutally beaten and left to die on a wire fence near Laramie, Wyoming. In the sermon titled "No More Scapegoats,"[18] Reverend Dr. Thomas Troeger names the oppressions challenging our American society and church for the last forty years: racism, sexism, and heterosexism. Dr. Troeger also includes significant events throughout the centuries in which Christianity has played a role as oppressor. The sermon is aural in form — written for the ear more than the eye. The Scripture lesson for this sermon is Luke 8:26–39, where Jesus heals the Gerasene Demoniac. Dr. Troeger preached this at St. John's Episcopal Cathedral in Denver.

---

18. Thomas H. Troeger, "No More Scapegoats," 1998. Reprinted with permission of the author, who was then the vice president and dean of Academic Affairs, Peck professor of Preaching and Communications, Iliff School of Theology, Denver, and is now the Professor of Christian Communications, Yale Divinity School, New Haven.

Sermon:
"NO MORE SCAPEGOATS"
by Thomas H. Troeger

Text: Luke 8:26–39

When I was in grade school
we often played a favorite game during recess.
Some of us would form a circle,
holding hands, facing outward.
All the others would stand in a larger circle,
about twenty-five feet away
from the inner circle.

The inner circle would chant:
"You're out, you're out,
you can't come in!
You're out, you're out,
you can't come in!"

Then the outer circle would charge,
trying to break into the inner circle.

"You're out, you're out,
you can't come in!
You're out, you're out,
you can't come in!"

It may be a game that starts in childhood.
But it continues for the rest of our lives.

"You're out, you're out,
you can't come in!
You're out, you're out,
you can't come in!"

We hear it chanted
to the gays and lesbians.
We hear it chanted
to the Jews
during the Nazi holocaust
and the pogroms of the medieval church.

We hear it chanted
to the African Americans
seeking freedom and equality.

We hear it chanted
to the women
seeking the vote
and the recognition of their full humanity.

We hear it chanted
to the first scientists
seeking new understanding of the physical world.

And very often
those who have led the chant
claimed to be Christian
and raised the dreadful chorus
in the name of God.

"You're out, you're out,
you can't come in!
You're out, you're out,
you can't come in!"

We hear it chanted
to the man possessed by demons
in our gospel lesson from Luke.

The man was naked
and lived among the tombs.

His community had tightened their circle
to keep him out.

He is not like us.
He is the mad one.
The sick one.
The crazy one.
The unnatural one.
The misfit.
He is the utterly other.

There is a technical term for this from cultural anthropology:
Deviance labeling.

Deviance labeling
is a way for us to escape
dealing with our own fears and angers.
We heap our projected fears
upon those who are different from us.

They become scapegoats.
We make them bear our demons for us.

And because there are so many of these demons
their name is "Legion,"
which is exactly the name given to them
in the biblical story.

A legion in the Roman empire
was a battle force
of four to six thousand soldiers.

Calling the demon "Legion"
suggests that there is nothing inherently wrong with the man
      himself.
He has been invaded
by demons not of his own making.

Luke tells us,
when the community saw the man
clothed, sitting at the feet of Jesus
and in his right mind,
They were afraid.

What were they afraid of?
If the man himself
had been the problem,
then they would have nothing to fear.
He was in his right mind now.

They were afraid
because the man
could no longer be their scapegoat.

They were afraid
because their neat and simplistic world
of who is in and who is out
had vanished.
They were afraid
because their deviance labeling
would now have to end.

They were afraid
because they could no longer
project phobias upon the man.

They were afraid
because now they would have to acknowledge
that it is the whole community
in need of exorcism.

The man begs to follow Jesus.
But Jesus won't let him.
Jesus says:
"Go home and tell what God has done for you."

The man is to be reintegrated into the community.
And the community is to come to terms
with its demons,
with its fears,
its hatreds,
its projected self-anger,
its deviance labeling.

There are to be no more scapegoats,
no more sacrificing of people
who are different from them.

I don't know what happened
when the man returned home.
Did that community finally
come to terms with its legion of demons?
Luke never tells us.

But we know this,
two thousand years after Christ,
our communities are still chanting,
"You're out, you're out,
you can't come in!
You're out, you're out,
you can't come in!"

We are still making scapegoats.
We are still excluding and projecting
our fears on others.

And what has that two thousand years gotten us?
Holy wars.
Violence.
Prejudice.
Hate crimes,
like the murder of Matthew Shepard.

I say let's try two thousand years of grace.
For two thousand years
let the human race
live by a new chant:
"You're in, you're in,
you're never out!
You're in, you're in,
You're never out!"

Sometimes when I suggest this,
people tell me I am morally lax.
"You have to draw the line somewhere,"
they say.

Of course
you have to draw one somewhere,
but let's draw it
where the prophet Micah draws the line:
"We are to love mercy,
do justice,
and walk humbly with our God."
Let's draw the line where
Jesus Christ draws the line:
"Love God with all that you are,
and love your neighbor as yourself."

I say draw the line there
and try two thousand years of grace.

When the Day of Judgment comes
the one whose mercy
is from everlasting to everlasting
is not going to say:
"The problem with you human beings
is you were too gracious.
You showed too much acceptance for one another."

In Rite I of the Book of Common Prayer
we pray how Christ made of himself
"a full, perfect and sufficient sacrifice."

Since Christ is
a full, perfect and sufficient sacrifice,
no one else is ever again
to be sacrificed.

No more scapegoats
No more chanting:
"You're out, you're out,
you can't come in!

I recall one particular day
we played that game in the school yard.
I was probably in the second grade.

My best friend was a girl named Louise.
We called her Weaser.

She was holding hands
in the inner circle.
She knew I was not fast
and I seldom made it into the circle.
She winked at me and nodded to me
to run toward her
when the charge began.

The inner circle started chanting:
"You're out, you're out,
you can't come in!
You're out, you're out,
you can't come in!"

I charged.
Weaser loosened her hand,
and I was in.

Immediately the boy next to her cried out,
"You do that and everybody will get in."

Weaser smiled,
and said with a sense of deep delight,
"Yeeeeeah!"
God is like Weaser!

Analysis

This sermon shows the biblical and historical prejudice toward the other (be they Jews, African Americans, women, or lesbians and gay men). It calls us to examine the way we regard one another (an-other) and all oppressed people in light of the death of Matthew Shepard. At various times throughout history, our Christian faith and biblical interpretation have lead humanity to cruel acts of exclusion. Usually it has been people with power and privileges in the church determining who is in and who is out of the church. Through our preaching, we can help congregations see and understand the biblical precedent in another light — one that radiates grace and inclusion, as Troeger's sermon does. Without using terms like homophobia or heterosexism, he is able to identify oppressive forces like deviance labeling or scapegoating as methods used to exclude people from community. Dr. Troeger's biblical interpretation of Luke's account of the man possessed by demons is that Jesus changes this man by welcoming him, and pointing out it was the community that projected their fears and demons onto him.

Some of Troeger's theological underpinnings for this interpretation are in the Episcopal Book of Common Prayer, a tradition that sees Christ as the perfect sacrifice, for which reason we have no cause to sacrifice anyone else ever again. Written and preached in a poetic fashion with simple sentences and using a childhood game to illustrate what is possible, Troeger imagines for the hearers a community that does not draw lines but welcomes all. His imaging God as Weaser draws attention away from stereotypical images of God as judge or father and replaces it with a new image, one from whom those once rejected may feel a welcome. Preached at a memorial service in the height of crisis, specifically within the LGBT community, Troeger's sermon demonstrates a passion for inclusion. It exemplifies both crisis preaching and preaching for the inclusion of LGBT people within the Christian church. In it, he names Matthew Shepard's senseless death, along with all other deaths throughout history that have been perpetrated in an effort to keep some people out.

In this chapter, I have explored the concept of coming out along with homophobia and heterosexism in the Christian church. The process of coming out is like an epiphany — a personal epiphany or revelation about one's self that is a sign of God's manifestation within us. With this new awareness, we can begin looking at how we define God, how we think about the Divine. What images of God do we have and what works for our understanding of the world once we have self-identified as a member of the lesbian, gay, bisexual, and transgender community? The coming out experience is in itself a transformative process, and as such leads us to reconsider traditional theological concepts.

Chapter 3

The Bible Comes Out

By the third century CE, both the Hebrew Scriptures and the books of the New Testament had been gathered into the biblical canon called the Bible and declared to be the guiding authority of the church. The inclusion of some Scriptures was contentiously debated for years, and indeed Christians continue to struggle with how to interpret what is contained within its pages. Thus, the Bible both unites and divides people of faith. It unites us by its very nature as the historical witness to the living God, through which we are linked across the millennia and distance, yet its interpretation has divided many who hold the Bible as central to their faith. The same can be said for its use in preaching: it is central to our homiletical task, yet diverse perspectives on it create division. In the LGBT community we are keenly aware of how the Bible is used to divide. For the purposes of developing a lesbian and gay homiletic, we acknowledge the dual role of the Bible, and know also that it, along with our faith, is what unites us in our common efforts. This chapter shows how the swords of biblical interpretation against queer people can be turned into plowshares, and the "spears into pruning hooks" (Micah 4:3).

This chapter examines the history of how the Bible has been used as a tool to oppress LGBT people. An introduction of several hermeneutical possibilities for reading the Bible through the eyes and lives of LGBT people will shift the focus toward preaching. Biblical scholarship by out LGBT professors and ministers is a growing field, and its contributions are exciting. While this book cannot cover all of the new developments in biblical study, as an example I will discuss at length one commentary on the book of Esther that I find particularly intriguing for the LGBT homiletic. It is a postmodern commentary that addresses issues of gender, identity, and ethnicity. But first, a recounting of how the Bible is used with different interests at heart.

It's no secret that the Bible is often used to condemn homosexuality. In fact, it is a primary weapon used against lesbians and gay men. Yet there are no verses in the Bible with the word "homosexuality" in them, nor was there in the ancient biblical world an understanding of homosexuality as a lifelong same-sex attraction. There are only a few references to sexual activity between people of the same gender, usually with the assumption that these are heterosexual people acting contrary to their nature.[1] Those who would use the Bible to denounce homosexuality have a completely different way of interpreting the Bible than those who do not denounce same-gender relationships. In many instances, an interpretation of the Bible that portrays same-sex attraction as antithetical to Christian or Jewish faith also interprets the Bible in a similar way on other topics. Over the course of human history, the Bible has been used to support slavery of African Americans by White Christian masters, to condone male hierarchy over women and violence against women, to promote hatred toward Jewish people, to start and sustain wars, and to teach and reinforce child discipline that is abusive. It has been used to sustain just about any prejudice or particular opinion.

Church historian Martin E. Marty is curious about this biblical practice when he writes in the *Christian Century,* "My friends are bemused by what they call the 'hermeneutical' issue: why the six or seven inches of print in the biblical testaments that condemn man-with-man and woman-with-woman sexual relations gets treated 'literally' while the much more strenuous Jesus-of-the-gospel strictures against divorce are not treated in the same way by most denominations."[2] Indeed, the

---

1. The Scriptures I am referring to here are: Genesis 19:1–28; Leviticus 18:22; 20:13; Romans 1:26–28; 1 Corinthians 6:9; 1 Timothy 1:10. These are often referred to as our "texts of terror" or the "clobber passages" used against homosexuals.

2. Martin E. Marty, "Ordained by Baptism," *Christian Century,* March 9, 2004, 55.

Bible can be and is interpreted in many different ways, and as regards homosexuals, it is often used in harmful ways.

The Bible is the central text of our faith, the history of our people, and our story to tell, too! Despite the harmful and vengeful interpretations of it against us, as out gay and lesbian preachers of the Gospel, our starting place remains the Bible. But we have twice the work to do to unmask the heterosexism pervasive in biblical commentaries and congregations and find our voices. In so doing, we strive to create biblical interpretation that is meaningful for our lives. Our sermons vary greatly depending on our particular context, the congregation's particular mix of people, the particular world events pressing in on us, and each particular preacher's self-awareness. In this way it is the same task that straight preachers have when preaching. Twentieth-century neo-orthodox Protestant theologian Karl Barth over fifty years ago defined preaching: "Preaching is the Word of God which he himself has spoken; but he makes use, according to his good pleasure, of the ministry of a man who speaks to his fellowmen, in God's name, by means of a passage from Scripture."[3] Thus, the Bible, as the Word of God, is as central to preaching for out LGBT clergy and in welcoming churches as it is for straight clergy.

What Is Hermeneutics?

Yet certain biblical texts have been and continue to be used in harmful ways against many LGBT people, to exclude, condemn, and cut them off from Christian fellowship based on references to homoerotic behavior in the text. A different understanding can liberate this biblical exegesis and move beyond a literal focus. We will not "use" the Bible for our "agenda" or for prooftexting, though everyone is guilty of this from time to time. As Christians, our aim is to preach the gospel, not the lectionary, or the Bible, or "queer life." We need a way to discern and interpret the Bible for ourselves, so that our lives are heard,

---

3. Karl Barth, *The Preaching of the Gospel* (Philadelphia: Westminster, 1963), 9.

while God's unconditional love and call to live justly come through our sermons. Hermeneutics, as the "art of understanding, refers to the methods and techniques used to make a text understandable in a world different from the one in which the text originated."[4] Usually readers and preachers of the biblical text identify with the chosen ones in the passage, the ones on the side of God, and not with those who are sinful or estranged from God. By contrast, a hermeneutics of suspicion asks what is not there in the text, as well as what the larger context is for the Scripture story. Furthermore, we know that the text interprets the reader; we also come to the text from a particular social location, and that affects how we interpret it. Depending on who exegetes a text and what method she or he employs, the message of Scripture will vary.

For example, exegesis done by LGBT clergy will yield new perspectives on Scripture because of our experience of living on the margin, in the closet, or invisible in the church. Eyes, ears, hearts, and spirits that have life experiences of rejection, discrimination, alienation, and condemnation will hear the Word of God in ways unlike those who have always been front and center with power and voice. Also, our very difference is sexual practice, and so the way we view life and the Scripture will naturally highlight possible sexual tones that have not previously been considered. For example, Nancy Wilson, leader of the Metropolitan Community Churches, considers several exegetical studies from a lesbian perspective, including that found in the book of Ruth. Ruth's commitment statement to Naomi is used at weddings to this day: "Where you go I will go; Where you lodge I will lodge; Your people shall be my people; and your God my God" (Ruth 1:6). Ruth's commitment to Naomi involves moving to a strange country, learning new customs, and eventually bringing forth new life by the birth of a child. Naomi's kin, Boaz, provides for progeny, and their son Obed becomes the father of Jesse, the father of David. Wilson sees the

---

4. *Concise Encyclopedia of Preaching*, ed. William H. Willimon and Richard Lischer (Louisville: Westminster John Knox Press, 1995), 175.

story this way: "Ruth takes the role of husband and of son to Naomi, by giving her a son. Ruth is Naomi's redeemer, providing her with a child to care for in her old age, preventing her from being cut off."[5]

By reading the text through the lenses of a lesbian, Wilson is claiming a place in the biblical canon that mirrors certain aspects of lesbian lives, like finding a way to live in a culture that is unfriendly to women, or creatively procreating to ensure continued survival, or one woman being the sole provider for two. Wilson calls this hermeneutic "outing the Bible." She wants us to assume there are and have always been gay men, lesbians, bisexuals, and transgender people in the biblical story, following Moses and Miriam in the desert, following Jesus into Jerusalem, meeting with the disciples in the upper room. She justifies this queer reading of the Bible like this: "Centuries of silence in biblical commentaries and reference books have not been fair. A passionate search for biblical truth about sexuality must be undertaken."[6] I suggest our preaching engage in this search for biblical truth about sexuality.

History Teaches: African Americans, Women, and Children

Indeed, other groups of people have sought to find their place in the Bible too. When African Americans faced slavery and white Christian slaveholders enforced the law with their exegesis of the Bible, blacks struggled to locate their place in Scripture. The Exodus story of the Israelites coming out from slavery in Egypt became a major source of comfort and support for their journey out of slavery. Many of the gospel songs by African Americans describe Israel crossing the Red Sea and journeying to the Promised Land, or speak of Jesus as friend and

---

5. Nancy L. Wilson, *Our Tribe: Queer Folks, God, Jesus, and the Bible* (San Francisco: HarperSanFrancisco, 1993), 155.
6. Ibid., 112.

close companion.[7] The study of God by African Americans calls into question the assumption that God is white. Professor and theologian James Cone's book *God of the Oppressed* introduced black liberation theology in 1975. His approach began with the black experience as a source of theology, then moved to an examination of "dominant" theology and how it excluded blacks. His work, which continues to deepen our understanding of God and challenge white racism, asked if God, even Jesus, is black.[8] This is the approach women took when they began addressing the absence of women's experience in theology.

Biblical study by, for, and about women resulted in womanist and feminist theologies. The term "Womanist" comes from Alice Walker's book *In Search of Our Mother's Garden* and has been appropriated by many women in church and society as a way of affirming themselves as black while simultaneously owning their connection with feminism and with the African American community. Walker herself makes this analogy, "Womanist is to feminist as purple is to lavender."[9] Feminist theology begins with women claiming and naming our own experiences and exploring the ways in which these discoveries might affect traditional theology. Uncovering the voices of Sara, Hagar, Rachel, Leah, Rebecca, Deborah, Miriam, and other biblical women, many of them unnamed, brings new perspectives on who God is and how God is among us. Imaging God as also female rather than only male, and the Christ as Christa, challenges the idolatry of one gender. Feminist theologian Mary Daly starkly sums up the problem of referring to God only in masculine terms, "If God is male, then male is God."[10] In the 1970s when Daly wrote that, she also challenged women to go deeper than just changing the pronouns for God; she advocated for the change to take place in our very being, our self-image. To trust

---

7. Gospel songs with titles like, "Go Down Moses," "We Shall Overcome," "Steal Away," "I've Got Peace Like a River," "Precious Lord, Take My Hand," and "Hush, Hush, Somebody's Calling My Name."

8. James H. Cone, *God of the Oppressed* (New York: Seabury Press, 1975), 133.

9. Alice Walker, *In Search of Our Mothers' Gardens* (New York: Harcourt Brace Jovanovich, 1984), xii.

10. Mary Daly, *Beyond God the Father* (Boston: Beacon Press, 1973), 19.

our experience of being a woman engages us in theological reflection rather than being defined by a patriarchal society.

With regard to using the Bible to support physical discipline of children, author and professor Philip Greven has written extensively on the biblical roots of corporal punishment in the rearing of children. Both the Old and New Testaments are sources for justification for physical discipline and punishment of children. Only in the last half of the twentieth century did we consider this child abuse. We now have laws preventing parents or caregivers from using children as slaves or forced laborers. Certain Scripture passages have been used to sustain reasons for physical punishment. The book of Proverbs has many passages that direct parents' treatment of their children, the most familiar and oft repeated being "Spare the rod, spoil the child" (Proverbs 13:24; 23:13–14). Jesus' teachings on children clearly do not support any kind of physical discipline by parents. On the contrary, Jesus teaches compassionate concern for children, encouraging the disciples and others to treat children as he did (Matthew 18:1–6). Though the Gospels do not favor child abuse, the key text in the New Testament that is cited to support harsh physical discipline of children is Hebrews 12:5–11. The text uses father and son references with phrases like "chastening of the Lord," "enduring chastening," and "fathers in flesh which corrected us." The father/son relationship that parallels God and Jesus is also seen by feminists as divine child abuse — Jesus the son who is sent by his father to die on a cross.[11] One version of the Christian story might be read as a father God who gives birth to a son by a virgin and the son later dies upon a cross while the father God does not rescue or stop this action. In this case, it seems ironic that this God who is all powerful and all knowing would intentionally let his son, who has done no wrong, die. Sorting through these biblical interpretations today that have supported child abuse in

---

11. Rita Nakashima Brock, *Journeys by Heart: A Christology of Erotic Power* (New York: Crossroad, 1988).

the past, it is astounding that the human community did not see its error sooner.

Liberation

Biblical hermeneutics from the particular experience of women, children, and African Americans challenges traditional interpretation of the Bible. Beginning with human experience and moving to the activity of God and Jesus within the larger human community, we can learn what is useful in creating a biblical hermeneutic that serves the LGBT community. While some biblical interpretations do indeed justify heterosexism and homophobia, the task of the Christian church is to reinterpret the texts of terror for LGBT in the face of such injustice and oppression. Throughout our human history, Christians from different locations used Scripture to support their own agendas. They have seen themselves as the favored ones, the chosen. In this way, women, children, foreigners, homosexuals — list whichever groups you wish — have at various times been systematically denigrated and excluded from God's favor. For example, that God is uniquely heterosexual is a byproduct of one group of people placing their prejudice, power, and position of majority over the other.

Thus, in order for the LGBT community to find its way out of the oppressive cycle of being "studied to death" by well-meaning Christian committees, or denied ordination or job placement, we must begin to imagine God, Jesus the Christ, the Holy Spirit, and other sources of theological meaning from within our own sexual orientation, our own lived experience. This is the starting place for all the liberation theologies mentioned above.

One of the first such efforts at constructing a queer biblical hermeneutic that reflects the diversity within the LGBT community is *Take Back the Word: A Queer Reading of the Bible.*[12] Twenty-one contributing essayists from Jewish, Christian, and Unitarian perspectives here offer

---

12. Robert E. Goss and Mona West, eds., *Take Back the Word: A Queer Reading of the Bible* (Cleveland: Pilgrim Press, 2000).

their unique reading of the biblical texts. This collection reflects the growing number of out LGBT people in faith communities and their courage to write and speak out as well. It is an excellent source for preachers, both queer and straight, as we continue to build an LGBT homiletic. In addition this homiletic will listen to the voices in the pews and those who have left the church.

Jesus Loves Us

The LGBT Christians who grew up singing "Jesus loves me, this I know, for the Bible tells me so..." most likely experienced a faithful, life-giving community within the church as children. Later in life, though, we have been hard pressed to find welcoming churches, even when signs hanging outside of churches read: "All Are Welcome" or "Open Hearts, Open Minds, Open Doors."[13] We learn as we come out to ourselves and to our families and friends that there are only a few Christians, and sometimes none, who welcome us as Jesus does. While those who are against us point to the Bible as justification for their hate, violence, and rejection, we must reclaim the truth of "Jesus loves us, this we know, for the Bible tells us so...." Certainly, the Bible and the God to whom it points are actually sources of redemption — and indeed serious commentary of this nature by lesbian and gay Christian theologians already exists. However, we must listen to their work, listen to the lives of LGBT people, and integrate these understandings into our preaching. Today there are many out lesbian and gay Christians who share their coming out stories, who listen deeply to the message of God's love, and who have returned to the church, albeit with more passion for justice. While knowing and listening to these Christians is important to our ministry of preaching, we also need a method by which we can study Scripture.

---

13. United Methodist Church slogan appearing on churches, literature, and buildings can be found at *www.umc.org/site/c.gjJTJbMUIuE/b.484771/k.CBA1/Home.htm.*

Coming Out as a Hermeneutic

Author and out gay Christian Chris Glaser uses the concept of "coming out" as his hermeneutic lens for reading the Bible. Glaser sees "coming out" as the paradigmatic experience that bonds gay men and lesbians and through which we can examine Scripture. He believes the coming out experience is a source of vulnerability that allows for God's self-disclosure. Glaser applies a "coming out" lens as a hermeneutical method to major themes in the Bible. His results yield hopeful interpretations for those who have been unable to identify with the traditional interpretation of biblical stories or characters. Traditional biblical interpretation has studied Scripture through primarily heterosexual or closeted models of being. Also absent from traditional biblical interpretation is the gift of sexuality. Either because of our Puritan heritage or our fear of sexuality, until recently Christians in the United States have resisted teaching and talking about sexuality within the church. Much to our surprise, the coming out of gay, lesbian, bisexual, and transgender Christians is drawing attention to sexuality despite the resistance of some Christians in the pews. These changes have thrown our denominations into a tailspin, rushing to catch up with current understandings of sexuality. Our lack of honest conversation and biblical teaching has left us without resources to have open dialogue about sexual expression and difference. Glaser's study is a bold and fresh look at familiar stories within Scripture with the approaches that are instructional in our preaching. Below is my summary of nine biblical themes seen through this lens in his book, *Coming Out as a Sacrament*; perhaps they will be inspiration for others to read the biblical text creatively within our community:

1. The garden in Genesis (Genesis 3). Coming out of innocence and shame to enjoy our bodies and sexual pleasure is radically different than focusing on sin and punishment.

2. Joseph and his coat of many colors (Genesis 37; 39–50). Coming out as a dreamer, a person with a special gift; we come out as

"gay" or "queer" and have special gifts. Joseph's special long-sleeved coat is sometimes referred to as a coat of many colors — a rainbow robe — a promise that difference is not always wrong.

3. The exodus from Egypt (Exodus). The Israelites' coming out of Egypt parallels our coming out experience; a release from the captivity of heterosexism is a joyous experience, but then we are faced with possible death in the desert, no real home, no road map to follow. We start wanting to go back to Egypt, the closet, where at least we felt safe and had food to eat.

4. Leaving the wilderness (Numbers 13; 14). Moses and the Israelites got close to the Promised Land (milk and honey), but they did not think they could conquer those who were living there, so they stayed by an oasis in the desert, deciding to settle for less. LGBT Christians are told to wait and be patient for full inclusion, but this will not prompt change. It is agitation and discomfort, not complacency, that bring about change. It's hard being out of the closet and working for change.

5. Coming out to love. No biblical passage actually affirms homosexuality in the strictest sense, but David and Jonathan's love and passionate devotion (1 and 2 Samuel) provide an example of a deeply committed relationship, as do Ruth and Naomi's loyalty and devotion (the book of Ruth). These relationships may not be sexual, but what justifies any relationship is not sex but love.

6. Coming out of privilege (Esther). The beautiful second queen, who is secretly Jewish in a Persian culture, comes out of her privilege to identify with her people in order to save them from a decree of death. She asks her people to fast in solidarity with her as she risks her life before the king, thus mirroring queer people who can pass as heterosexuals and yet give up their privilege in society and come out.

7. Coming out of anger (Jonah). Jonah is the reluctant prophet who learns the hard way what God intends for him to do after

running away the first time. Jonah is called to preach repentance to the Ninevites — the very people oppressing Jonah's people. When the Ninevites repent, Jonah becomes angry because they received the same mercy and grace as the Israelites, and Jonah didn't want to share this with his oppressors. Yet God is even the God of our oppressors — a theme of universalism often found in the prophets. The same God in whose image we are created as LGBT people is the same God of the Christian Coalition, which actively persecutes us today. We must not forget to offer our oppressors opportunities to turn from their shameful ways and receive God's mercy and grace.

8. Coming out of "traditional family values." Jesus ignored his family's departure from Jerusalem to go and sit in the temple, his "Father's house" (Luke 2:49); he left his family, never married, and as far as we know, never had children; he called his disciples away from their families (Luke 9:59–62), told them he had no home (Luke 9:57), and claimed his message would set families against one another (Matthew 10:35–36). Jesus was hardly the supporter of the so-called traditional family values, meaning one man, one woman, and some children. Instead, Jesus extended the meaning of family by calling anyone who does the will of God his brother, sister, and mother (Mark 3:35). Jesus defended the eunuchs — traditionally outcasts — by drawing a circle that included them.

9. Coming out as ourselves (John 4:1–42). Jesus' conversation with the Samaritan woman at the well is just one example of the way Jesus did not follow traditional societal norms for religion, race, gender, and morality — he spoke to a Samaritan woman who had five husbands! By offering her living waters — acceptance and hope for a new way of living — she was transformed. Jesus' encounter with this woman illustrates the call to right relationship with God. When we seek transformation of ourselves we

find Jesus calling to us, repeating: God loves us, God loves us, and God loves us.

Round Table Hermeneutic

Another hermeneutical method arises out of biblical stories in dialogue with the human community, especially those who are often without voice. The emphasis here is a dialogue between the historical stories about God's involvement in human history and with people's lives in the pew. Whether the sermon starts with the Bible or the life of the congregation, it's the conversation that matters. The late author and preacher Lucy Atkinson Rose illustrated this method with the image of a round table.[14] A round table, she explained, does not allow for any one person to be the "head" of the rest and allows all seated to see each other, as opposed to one person in front of the students who all face forward. The biblical text is read and put on the table for all to hear, see, and comment on. This round table church is nonhierarchical and communal in its relationship between the preacher and her congregation. At the "roundtable" all people are equal in God's eyes and equal in status in the community. Of special note are those who have not usually been welcomed at the table; those who are invisible like the poor or lesbian and gay people; and those we do not typically find in the church (the homeless, those with mental illnesses, or immigrants). The empty chair is a reminder of those missing from our human community. This is not only a place for talking, but a place for listening to the other. Here, through intentional listening, all members can begin to equalize power within the community. Those on the margin find a place to be heard. Those with the loudest voice or who are most often heard (the preacher) are called to listen. This hermeneutical method could be especially useful among out LGBT clergy since

14. Lucy Atkinson Rose, *Sharing the Word: Preaching in the Roundtable Church* (Louisville: Westminster John Knox Press, 1997).

our voices have either been ignored or shamed into silence within the church.

The Bible's themes of God's grace, love, and liberating truth are central to preaching for LGBT clergy and welcoming churches. There are many, many biblical stories that, when read through the lenses of LGBT people, will offer a word of hope to all God's people, not just the queer community. LGBT preachers will preach with an intensity and passion about God's gift of love and the call to choose life, because, like Lazarus in the grave, we experienced death in the closet.[15] When, and if, we have a community to call us as Jesus called Lazarus to life, "Come out!" we will preach with the experience of resurrection. No scriptural text will be beyond our hermeneutic, but some will make more sense to us than others.

A Biblical Model

Having explored several hermeneutical methods, I want to look specifically at the book of Esther, as I establish a homiletical method. There are several books in the Bible that remain unexplored in the Christian community because preachers or theologians have found less "Christian" content in them; for example, the Song of Solomon, Obadiah, Nahum, and Haggai. The book of Esther falls into this category even though in recent years it has gained some measure of popularity. Esther is part of the Wisdom literature of Hebrew Scripture. The Reformation theologian, Martin Luther, in *Table Talk*, confessed that Esther "Judaizes" too much and is full of "pagan naughtiness."[16] Other Christian commentaries have also had trouble finding ways to interpret the story to be useful in supporting the Christian message of salvation through Jesus the Christ.

---

15. Being in the closet about one's sexual orientation or preference or gender identity can be compared to being in a grave, a place of no light or life.

16. Carol M. Bechtel, *Interpretation Series: Esther* (Louisville: Westminster John Knox Press, 2002), 16.

The Esther Story

The biblical book of Esther tells a story of beauty queens, palace intrigue, different faiths, courage, and attempted genocide. In the story, King Ahasuerus is married to Queen Vashti, whom he discards after she rejects his offer to appear naked in front of his friends during a feast. The exiled Jew, Mordecai, has adopted his cousin's orphaned girl named Hadassah and raised her. She is selected from the candidates to be Ahasuerus's new wife and assumes the "throne name" of Esther. The king's prime minister, Haman (an Agagite or non-Jew), and Haman's wife, Zeresh, plot to have King Ahasuerus kill all the Jews, without knowing that Esther is Jewish. Encouraged by Mordecai, Esther saves the day for her people: at the risk of endangering her own safety, she warns Ahasuerus of Haman's plot to kill all the Jews. Haman and his sons are hanged on the fifty-cubit stake he built for Mordecai, and Mordecai becomes prime minister in Haman's place. However, Ahasuerus's edict decreeing the murder of the Jews cannot be rescinded, so he issues another edict allowing the Jews to take up arms and kill their enemies, which they do.

My interest in Esther is to claim the story of a Jewish queen who can serve as a preaching model for gay, lesbian, bisexual, and transgender clergy in our practice of ministry. She also serves as a model for straight clergy who come out of their heterosexual privilege on behalf of their lesbian sisters and gay brothers, thus risking acceptability in their congregations. The Jewish Queen Esther speaks truth to power, risking her life and saving her people. Like other prophets of the Old Testament, she rises to the occasion on wings of faith and courage. Think of Nathan's parable to King David after his sin with Bathsheba and murder of Uriah. Nathan must give up his personal need for safety for the greater good of speaking the truth to his king (2 Samuel 12:1–15). Think of another murderer — Naboth, a powerless vegetable gardener and an Israelite, whose refusal to give up his vineyard to King Ahab results in his death. The prophet Elijah enters the story an outsider who has no investment in this king's power, and who must bring God's truth to King Ahab (1 Kings 21). These biblical stories of speaking truth to power are one form of preaching. Speaking truth to power is also complicated. Whose "truth" does one speak? Who has the "power" and who does not? How does the speaking-truth-to-power preacher determine answers to these questions? The biblical texts and our congregation are multilayered, and so are we! Preacher, professor, and priest/prophet Walter Brueggemann describes his preaching function as that of a Preacher-Scribe who functions like a pastoral therapist, but in the pulpit. He writes:

> Like a therapist, the Preacher-Scribe does not own the text; the text lives in, with, and under the memory of the community. So the Preacher-Scribe gets out of the center and out of the way. The Preacher-Scribe trusts the text to have a say through the power of the Spirit rather than the power of the preacher; trusts the listening congregation to make the connections it is able to make; and trusts the deep places of truthful power and powerful truth that draw us in and send us forth in repentance, a turn that makes all things new.[17]

Brueggemann's analysis of what both the text and the Spirit do in speaking truth to power can be seen in the story of Esther. She is a minority placed in a position of privilege and then is called upon to use that position to save others by coming out about her ethnicity. Furthermore, the story of Esther has specific implications for a lesbian and gay homiletic. The book of Esther is therefore an excellent choice for developing a lesbian and gay homiletic because of its multiple hermeneutical layers.

Esther Reigns

As regards the speaking-truth-to-power model of preaching, there are several ways in which Esther reigns for the LGBT community. First,

---

17. Anna Carter Florence, ed., *Inscribing the Text: Sermons and Prayers of Walter Brueggemann* (Minneapolis: Fortress Press, 2004), 18.

the story of Esther parallels that of most LGBT people, who can pass as straight (or in some instances as the expected gender), and who, by revealing their identity, come out as Esther did. Because some lesbians and gay men can "pass" as straight people, this can work either to their advantage or disadvantage, depending on their desired outcome. Therefore, coming out is about choosing not to pass anymore, about giving up the privilege of straight status, and about learning how to navigate being "out" in a straight society. This concept of passing is not unique; other cultures and genders have tried it. Remember the movie *Yentl*, when a woman poses as a man in order to study the Hebrew Scripture? She passed as a man in a culture that saw women as possessions with no ability to think critically or have a voice at God's table. Another example is African Americans who could pass as white people; they experienced the privileges a white society affords, but if their color was revealed, they could experience a backlash. Listen to the following narrative by an African American woman explaining the concept of passing:

> I can tell you about my own family. See, we were all colors. Not real dark, but we weren't all what you call blue veins. Some of them went as white, and some of them didn't. I have two cousins on my mama's side and two cousins on my daddy's side. They went to California and became white. Understand, now, my grandmother didn't go to the other side for good. She just did that in public. But she loved her family, dark or bright. My mama married a brown man. She worked as a white to get more money for her children. But, these cousins, I am telling you about; they are white now. We know they still living. But, they're strangers to us now. They married white people, their kids are white and they're lost to us. Either live with the degradations and racism that white people put on us or use your skin to an advantage. And that's what they did.[18]

---

18. Wendy Ann Gaudin, "Passing Narratives," *The History of Jim Crow*, online at *www.jimcrowhistory.org/resources/lessonplans/hs_es_passing_enarratives.htm*.

Covering is another form of hiding one's true nature or identity to avoid prejudice or certain penalties in society. Yale law professor and author Kenji Yoshino explains this concept using his life as a gay man and a Japanese American in his book *Covering: The Hidden Assault on Our Civil Rights*. "Covering" is distinguished from passing; "rather than trying to render a characteristic invisible, a person might manage or mute it. Franklin D. Roosevelt was an example: everyone knew he needed a wheelchair, but he would still have himself seated behind a table before a meeting."[19] Yoshino, who has come out to his parents, his friends, and his colleagues, feels the pressure to live as though being gay does not have too much effect on his life. He modifies his physical appearance and reduces his time in the gay culture as a way of covering his identity for others.

By contrast, an example of not covering and therefore being rejected by the dominant culture's expectations is evident in the ongoing debate about who can march in the St. Patrick's Day parade in New York City. A lesbian city council speaker wanted to wear a gay-pride pin in the parade, but the parade chairman would not allow it. Had she chosen not to wear an identifying pin she would have been allowed to march alongside her Irish counterparts. The parade chairman likened letting Irish gays and lesbians into the parade to neo-Nazis wanting to march in an Israeli parade or the Ku Klux Klan wanting to march in Harlem with African Americans.[20] While there may be an argument for the right to exclude certain identifications during a parade celebrating another identity, the comparison is grave. It shows why some LGBT people choose to pass or cover rather than face this kind of discrimination.

In addition to Esther passing as a Persian and then coming out as a Jew, this is also a story about living a faithful life in a culture that does not recognize her religious identification as such, and is even hostile to

19. Ann Althouse, "The Conformist," *New York Times Book Review,* January 22, 2006, 11.

20. Winnie Hu, "Council Speaker Won't March in Parade," *New York Times,* March 17, 2006.

her particular faith. LGBT Christians experience this marginalization within the church and face oppression similar to that of Esther and her uncle, Mordecai, who is also Jewish. A newer commentary on Esther suggests one possible audience for the Esther story: "The audience the book addresses appears to be the Jews who live in close proximity to foreign rulers and must learn to make their own way in a society in which they are a minority and in which there is always danger of persecution and oppression."[21] This sounds strangely familiar to me as a member of the LGBT community.

Commentary on Esther

Biblical scholar Timothy Beal's commentary on Esther, *The Book of Hiding,* is likewise a fascinating exploration of gender and ethnic identity in both the historical text of Esther and in our postmodern society. While the inclusion of Esther in the Bible may be debatable, Beal offers new insights as to why its inclusion is critical today. We live with questions of gender, ethnicity, and self-identity that are challenging long-held assumptions of what it means to be a person and to be in relation with another. Beal's contemporary theory concerning gender, ethnicity, and social location alongside the story of Esther leads readers to ask not why is Esther in the Bible, but "What does 'biblical' mean anyway?" In his book, Beal writes:

> One is inclined to ask, What kind of Scripture is this? God hiding, and a royal buffoon filling the space of divine retreat, no sign of religion or religious practice, no sacred space, Mount Sinai lost behind smoke and ashes, the Law of the Father illegible: What does this have to do with anything we commonly assume to be "biblical"? Everything. But not as an affirmation of those assumptions. Esther is present within the biblical canon as

---

21. Sidnie Ann White Crawford, *Esther: Women's Bible Commentary,* ed. Carol A. Newsom and Sharon H. Ringe (Louisville: Westminster John Knox Press, 1998), 131.

a kind of *fracture*, a fissure in the divinely ordained order established elsewhere, opened by the experience of exile and diaspora.
Indeed, I suggest that it be understood, like Job, Ecclesiastes, and
other biblical texts, as an *interrogation* of biblical authority from
within — a biblical self interrogation. I suggest that this is precisely why it must be embraced: because it allows us to [re]think
the limits of common, simplistic assumptions about "the biblical,"
and even about religious literature in general, which pervade
intellectual discourse today.[22]

Beal's remark about "God hiding" compels my attention as one
who understands something of what it means to hide. In the English
translation, this book of the Bible does not mention God; the Hebrew
word gives a clue as to why. Beal's uncovering of the Hebrew word
Esther, as meaning "I will hide," or "divine hiding," gives reason to
pause and consider the purpose of Esther in the whole narrative of
the Bible.[23] Esther is the only book in the entire Bible where God's
activity appears to be absent but is actually working through hidden
means. Beal makes a parallel between the book of Esther, which is
about Israel in exile, and our current social location in the aftermath
of Western civilization, a postmodern world.

Building on his analysis, Beal's commentary unearths many possible
ways one might read Esther. For instance, concerning the social location of who is an insider and who is an outsider, Beal notes Esther's rise
to a powerful position as queen, and a Jew in the Persian culture. Another way could be a power analysis of gender, ethnicity, and identity.
For instance, humans place value and power on one another according to gender, ethnicity, identity (social status), and sexual orientation.
In many instances in the Bible, when humans make one assumption
about people, God (or Jesus) makes a surprisingly different one. For
example, in the New Testament, Paul describes his understanding of

---

22. Timothy K. Beal, *The Book of Hiding: Gender, Ethnicity, Annihilation and Esther*
(London and New York: Routledge, 1997), 118.

23. Ibid., 117.

God's inclusive activity in Jesus in his letter to the Galatians. He defends the inclusion of those who are Abraham's offspring as well as the Gentiles who have faith, as he tries to unravel the mystery of law versus faith for the Galatian community. In the end of chapter 3 he offers this as a description of the new community that faith in Christ Jesus creates: "There is neither Jew nor Greek, slave nor free, male nor female, for you are all one in Christ Jesus" (Galatians 3:28). In effect, Paul eliminates barriers to faith in Christ by addressing the gender, ethnicity, and social status of people in his day. All, he says, are one in Christ Jesus. In contrast, in Esther, social status, gender, and ethnicity all play a role in the character's lives. The king is Persian and male, the queen is Jewish and female; the Persians are in power, the Israelites are a minority; men have power to rule and yet the female queen is able to persuade King Ahasuerus to use his power differently. God works through these human attributes to bring about the salvation of the Jews in this particular context. This, of course, does not answer the lingering question in the book of Esther about those who are killed as a result of the king's decree. It leaves us with the age-old question of omnipotence versus a universal loving creator.

Esther and Queer Folk

There are several parallels between the queer community and Esther: both are minorities in a majority culture, both risk their lives when they come out, and both have faith in God's abiding presence in their lives. In addition, the lives of many lesbian women, gay men, bisexual, and transgender Christians are invisible within the church, unless they have come out. God is present within the LGBT community even if the church is unable to receive and affirm this good news.

Concerning the parallels between Esther's story and LGBT people, Beal writes:

> For Esther and indeed for Mordecai too, Jewish identity can be hidden simply by choosing not to disclose it. In the ancient

text of Esther and in the modern discourse on homosexuality, the dynamics of hiding and disclosure, closeting and coming out, reflect a historical context of identity ambivalence, with regard to Jewish/non-Jewish identity on the one hand and homo/heterosexual identity on the other.[24]

Interweaving several other authors (Jean Racine, Marcel Proust, and Eve Kosofsky Sedgwick), Beal follows a line of thought about Jewish identity as a category of ethnicity not unlike homosexual identity. One chooses whether to disclose or hide one's ethnicity; depending on the culture, disclosure usually involves an unknown risk. Beal carries this analogy to the point of Esther's coming out party and how that could have ended very differently — she, rather than Haman, could have been on the gallows. As the LGBT community continues to come out in the church, it will result in making the church visibly out (more gay or queer friendly) and more inclusive. Perhaps this is threatening to the mainline denominations that for so long have denounced LGBT people, and kept us from fellowship. To recognize God within the individual and collective lives of queer people would require some admission of wrongdoing, but the church has not been quick to ask forgiveness when it has wronged others. The continual coming out of Christians, especially LGBT clergy, and straight clergy on behalf of LGBT people, will inevitably involve risk and loss. There will be those who lose their ordinations, their jobs, and their families, which must be taken into consideration. In Esther's case, speaking truth to power brought cause for celebration.

Celebration

The story of Esther is celebrated within the Jewish faith through a festival called Purim. This celebration of their survival calls for a party in which people wear costumes and masks like characters in the story,

---

24. Ibid., 111.

with most attention going to the pretty Queen Esther and the evil Haman. Beal suggests an even deeper meaning of Purim: "Purim is so preoccupied with themes of carnival and masquerade — with blurring identities and subverting traditional structures of authority and power."[25] The Jewish people celebrate their liberation from the death sentence with much singing, dancing, and feasting. For many it is a fun time when dressing up, acting out, and having a carnival or parade is encouraged.

This rings true within the gay and lesbian community, which has learned to celebrate and have fun in spite of the dangers and risks of coming out in this world — pride parades in June, drag shows, queer proms, debutante balls (coming out parties), and cross dressing. The LGBT community is wide and diverse. Organizations have pulled resources together to advocate, support, and advance rights, like the Human Rights Campaign, which created a day of the year in which "coming out" is celebrated and encouraged. It's called National Coming Out Day and is every October 11. Some congregations acknowledge this with a sermon and worship experience that recognizes and reflects on the lives of LGBT people. Others invite a gay chorus to provide music on that day. Worship resources have developed over time; for example, author Chris Glaser has written a prayer for National Coming Out Day, using the Esther story:

> Dear God, as a gay community we are divided by closets. Some of us are not known as gay, just as Esther was unknown to King Ahasuerus as a Jew. Some of us find "grace and favor" in the sight of those with power, and are tempted as Esther to keep quiet, even when our people are attacked. As Esther risked her life in solidarity with her people, celebrated now in the Jewish Festival of Purim, open the eyes of us all to the solidarity needed to protect the lives, rights, and livelihoods of our people. Redeem

---

25. Ibid., 1.

us by the solidarity modeled in Esther. May National Coming Out Day be our Purim.[26]

In summary, throughout the book of Esther, God is hiding, but when Esther comes out as a Jew she identifies her allegiance to God (Esther 4:17). In essence, she says, "Here I am — here's what it's really all about — God is in me." This is what gave life to the Jewish people and prevented them from being annihilated. Esther risked her life for her people by speaking truth to power, by naming who she is, and by being in a position of privilege as she did so. When a person or group says, "Here I am, here is where I live and breathe and have my being," then they are locating where God is in their lives. This is reminiscent of Moses and the burning bush. Moses asks, "Who will I say sent me?" The reply comes, "I am who I am," or "the great I am has sent you."[27] When a transgendered person, a gay man, or a lesbian woman can claim their identity with healthy self-respect, even pride, we need to hear that as a dwelling place for God — the great I AM WHO I AM. The declaration of self both names and liberates a person.

The Cultural "I AM"

Like Moses and Esther, there are people in our postmodern world who have lived the great "I Am" — the assurance that who they are matters and that their self-worth is not built on definitions others provide. Included in their lives is a message for us, not unlike Esther's.

Born in 1924, black feminist lesbian poet Audre Lorde grew up in Harlem and spent her life teaching and writing; her honest free verse gave a powerful witness about a black woman who loved women. When faced with breast cancer, Lorde reevaluated her life and became even more determined to have her words and speeches match her life. Writing of her mortality in her essay "The Transformation

26. Chris Glaser, *Coming Out to God: Prayers for Lesbians and Gay Men, Their Friends and Family* (Louisville: Westminster John Knox Press, 1991), 94–95.
27. My paraphrases of Exodus 3:13–15, NRSV.

of Silence into Language and Action," she says she regretted her silences most. "My silence had not protected me. Your silences will not protect you."[28] She believed that culture had silenced women, blacks, and lesbians specifically, but that all people could be silenced for one reason or another. Being silent about your truth in life will not protect you, even though it may feel safer. Coming out and being true to one's self — who one was created to be — energizes one's work and brings more life to all those around you. Speaking the truth about her life, Lorde's words and life inspired many women, lesbians and straight alike, to honor the truth of their lives and name themselves rather than letting society use derogatory labels. Rather than choosing to live an invisible life in the closet, Lorde claimed her identity.

In another country, around the globe, the same truth grew from an oppressive context. In South Africa, Nelson Mandela spent twenty-seven years in prison resisting apartheid in his country. His imprisonment is chronicled in his book *Long Walk to Freedom*.[29] Upon his release, the country elected him as the first black president of South Africa. In his inaugural speech in May 1994, he said, "Who am I to be brilliant, gorgeous, handsome, talented and fabulous? Actually, who are you not to be? You are a child of God. Your playing small does not serve the world. There is nothing enlightened about shrinking so that other people won't feel insecure around you. You were born to manifest the glory of God within."[30] His ability to keep his self-worth alive in that oppressive system and not become like his oppressors is nothing short of a miracle. Mandela knows the deep truth of God's grace and love for him and for all. White South Africans established their privilege over and against blacks based on the value of skin color,

28. Audre Lorde, *Sister Outsider* (Freedom, CA: Crossing Press Feminist Series, 1984), 41.

29. Nelson Mandela, *Long Walk to Freedom: The Autobiography of Nelson Mandela* (Boston: Bay Back Book, 1995).

30. Nelson Mandela, South African Presidential Inaugural Speech (quoting spiritual leader Marianne Williamson of the Church of Today, Detroit), May 1994. See *www.aetw.org/mandela.htm* on attributing this statement to Mandela.

yet Mandela's persistence witnesses to a higher truth — God's suffering and redemption. His speaking truth to power resulted in a long
prison sentence, but he was vindicated in the end.

In yet another example from those who have suffered on the margin of society, people living with HIV/AIDS created a graphic symbol
similar to the concept that silence does not support life. They needed
to support one another through the AIDS crisis in the 1980s, and
this simple equation made the point: SILENCE=DEATH. This was
to encourage people to come out about being gay or HIV-positive so
that the disease would not be spread as easily. It was also about speaking the truth to those in power: those making the drugs for HIV and
those in the government who were trying to ignore the AIDS epidemic
through limiting funds for research. Drawing on parallels to the Nazi
period, the logo became widely proclaimed and declared that "silence
about the oppression and annihilation of gay people, then and now,
must be broken as a matter of our survival."[31] However, since many
breakthroughs have occurred in HIV prevention and treatment, a new
logo has replaced the old one: ACTION=LIFE. The following reflection describes the transition of this symbol from SILENCE=DEATH
to ACTION=LIFE. It is on the occasion of the ordination of the first
openly gay bishop (the Reverend Gene Robinson, Episcopal Church)
by Rev. Jay E. Johnson at Pacific School of Religion. By the very nature of consecrating an openly gay bishop, our church and society have
moved from SILENCE=DEATH to ACTION=LIFE. It also names
Lorde's truth about silence as well as Esther's self-declaration.

> There is a price to pay for telling the truth, just as there is a price
> for remaining silent. Of course, there's more to human thriving
> than truthful speech — but there can't be less. Speaking the
> truth won't guarantee we'll live authentically — but there's no
> hope of doing so if we lie or keep silent. Nearly twenty years
> ago, AIDS activists reminded us that *silence equals death*. Not

---

31. *www.backspace.com/notes/2003/04/07/x.html.*

long after that they flipped that coin over and reminded us that *action equals life.*

Breaking the silence by speaking the truth is a form of action for the sake of life. Speech is action insofar as speaking the truth changes people — it changes both those who speak and those who listen. The words conversation and conversion come from the same root. The truth about the ways things are and about who we are tends to do that — it changes quite a lot.[32]

The Sermonic "I AM"

Speech, like preaching, changes people — both those who speak and those who listen. The truth telling that LGBT preachers have done in their lives already will show forth in their preaching as well. Sermons are a major source of revelation; where God comes out as LGBT, preachers witness to God's reconciling love. I am urging LGBT preachers not to come out personally through sermons, though that may happen, but to preach the presence of God by their faithful lives. What this hermeneutical exegesis of Esther offers us is a model of speaking truth to power, and through that God will come out in the sermon.

&

This next sermon is offered as an example of preaching to a congregation struggling with its heterosexism and homophobia following the coming out of their senior minister as a gay man. The congregation had already become an open and affirming congregation and hired a lesbian minister, but the news that their senior pastor was also gay came as quite a shock.

---

32. The Reverend Jay E. Johnson, Ph.D., Pacific School of Religion, Center for Lesbian and Gay Studies, Programming and Development Director. See online *www.clgs.org/7/johnson_erobinson_eordination. html#part2.*

Sermon:
"WHEAT OR WEEDS?"
by Olive Elaine Hinnant

Text: Matthew 13:24–30

The rabbi and well-known author Harold Kushner, whose first book, *When Bad Things Happen to Good People,* became a best-seller, has published a fairly new book titled *How Good Do We Have to Be? A New Understanding of Guilt and Forgiveness.*

Curious about just how good I, or anyone else, need to be, I finally got around to reading it recently. Kushner offers a different interpretation of the Adam and Eve story, which he notes was where our notions of right and wrong, good and evil got started in the Garden of Eden.[33] The snake tempted Eve, Eve tempted Adam, and they both ate of the fruit. One disobedient act resulted in banishment from paradise. Christianity knows this discourse as the doctrine of original sin. Paradise lost, and humanity tries dearly to regain it by creating states of utopia or purity, none of which ever succeed because humanity is doomed. But Kushner reads the story as an "inspiring, even liberating story, a story of what a wonderful, complicated, painful and rewarding thing it is to be a human being."

He suggests the "story of the Garden of Eden is a tale, not of Paradise Lost, but of Paradise Outgrown, not of Original Sin but of the birth of conscience."[34]

We begin with this as a background to hearing the parable this morning that refers to what is good and what is evil. In the telling of the parable, it seems that the good seed amounts to wheat and the bad seed is the weed. Easy enough.

---

33. Harold Kushner, *How Good Do We Have to Be? A New Understanding of Guilt and Forgiveness* (New York: Little, Brown, 1996), 21.
34. Ibid.

The poet John Milton writing more than three hundred years ago also saw this truth: "Good and evil, we know in the field of this world, grow up together."[35]

Matthew's telling of yet another parable about the final judgment for those who would be compared to weeds is evidence of his frustration with an early group of Christ-followers. They were not doing church the way he felt they should, and therefore, he announces through Jesus' parables that there will come a time when they will be punished for what they have done or not done.

Certainly, there are times when Matthew's vision speaks to our heartaches about being the church.[36] We get a good project going, maybe working with kids in an after-school program, and then along come new volunteers with new ideas and now everything is completely mixed up. Or we welcome new members only to find that their version of church differs from that of those who have been members for fifty years. Expectations of how church people are to behave vary from congregation to congregation, but there is always some evil and some good mixed in. Good and evil, they grow together in human soil.

The early church leaders expected Jesus to return soon and pronounce people as sinners and saints destined for different locations, but when Jesus did not return in bodily form, the church took it upon itself to become the judge of people. It stepped into God's place...moving into the position of judge on Earth; the church through the centuries has tried to pull weeds from within its ranks all

---

35. John Milton, *Areopagitica*, English Parliament Speech, June 16, 1643; see *www.stlawrenceinstitute.org*. John Milton published *Areopagitica* as an appeal to Parliament in their discussion of government control of censoring authors. He recognized that there needed to be some accountability, but felt the government had encroached on the freedom of thought, speech, and writing. This publication is often used in citing democratic values of freedom of speech. I felt this was an issue in this congregation as well, but did not name it directly in my sermon.

36. Thomas Troeger, *New Proclamation, Series A, 1999* (Augsburg: Fortress Press, 1999), 157.

the while condemning those who did not conform to truth as defined by those who wield power in the church.

Take, for example, the Crusades in the Middle Ages. Theologian Karen Armstrong has a new book about the crusades, holy wars, and jihads. Not only Christianity, but also Judaism and Islam have been, at times, responsible for ghastly acts in the name of truth.

Another example of this is the Vatican document in 2000 *Dominus Iesus,* which asserted that Christianity is the only true religion and that the Roman Catholic Church is the only true church within Christianity. It was an attempt to weed out and prevent further growth of ecumenical and interfaith relationships.

The Roman Catholic Church is not the only example. After 9/11, when many religious groups were pulling together to call upon God and witness to their faith in the midst of a national crisis, an interfaith event was held in New York City where religious leaders gathered for worship. The then president of the Missouri Synod Lutheran Church participated in that event. But following that service members of his denomination called for his resignation because he had been in worship with others who did not believe in Jesus Christ in the same way they did, and as a result he lost his job and a new policy was developed that prevents Missouri Synod leaders from participation in future interfaith events.

There is always the temptation to root out evil, to go on a crusade, to make life right as one understands it. Pulling weeds is therapeutic; it gives us a feeling of satisfaction — that we have done something worthwhile to protect the flowers, fruits, or veggies. Yet we try that in human soil and it doesn't work as well. Our attempts to eradicate evil on our own become evil in themselves. Whenever Christians try to eradicate evil we end up being self-righteous and cruel. Witch burnings and heretic burnings are signs of our attempts at religious purity. The aim to keep the church pure, with "wheat" only, always results in very strict and narrow circumstances.

Let both grow together, urges the land owner.

Let both grow together.

We can't purify ourselves, only God does.

Inevitably, no matter how good we try to be, we will be seen or found to be a weed at some time in our lives.

We are both weeds and wheat at different times and to different people.

God alone is the God of the harvest.

Only God knows our wheat days and our weed days.

Nature needs weeds. Gardeners know that weeds do a service by adding shade and stabilizing the soil and that weeds can be composted or used as mulch.

This is a reminder that in this universe there is a more complex order of God's creation, which despite all that we do know, is really beyond our knowing.

I would place my bets on God's judgment that gathers both the wheat and the weeds.

There is no difference — God gathers them all in because God is a God of life, of being and love.

As the psalmist wrote, "The darkness is a light to God."

Therefore, "The weeds are as wheat to God."

If one were to look back through the history of God's people, with the idea of wheat and weeds in mind, it would seem that God has a penchant for calling people who are on the outside, who have been evil, as we see it, or who are marginalized because of who they are.

In the Bible, Moses, the great leader of the Israelites, had murdered prior to the burning bush experience, and he continued to have trouble with his anger.

Think of Jacob, the thief and scoundrel who through his shady deals becomes Israel, the one who struggles with God and prevails.

Think of Hannah, the barren one, who was likely a weed in her family and destined for the compost pile. Yet when her prayer for a child is answered, she is restored to full communion.

Think of David, an unknown shepherd boy whose beauty and grace caught the eyes of Saul, who made him king, the king of

Israel. David, whose lust for beauty led him to commit adultery, then murder Bathsheba's husband, and try to hide his adultery.

David who loved Jonathan, and Jonathan who loved David more than a woman.

God sees what we cannot see. We know the brokenness of humanity all too well, but live as though perfection were the ultimate goal. Anyone who thinks they have God figured out, who has all the rules down and has memorized the Scriptures, is not likely to see God, to know God, to come face-to-face, unless they are willing to give up their self-righteousness. We are creatures of great deeds, great art, music, even heroism at times, and we are capable of designing death chambers, the death penalty, and death-dealing systems. We are a mixed breed. "Let them grow together until the harvest," says the landowner. What are we to do in the meantime? What are we to do with our wheat and weed potential? Just exercise it, as we need to? Just let it be?

Back to the story of Adam and Eve. Remember Kushner's interpretation is that the Garden of Eden is a tale, not of Paradise Lost, but of Paradise Outgrown, not of Original Sin but of the birth of conscience.

Excommunicated Catholic, now Episcopal priest, Matthew Fox calls this the Original Blessing, that our very humanity is a blessing not a curse, that our ability to be both wheat and weeds is the very glory of God's creation, that we are not meant to be perfect, but made whole in community. Out of the Garden of Eden, we come again, learning how painfully complex life is. We have knowledge that some things are good and others are bad. This also includes the ability to be strong enough to forgive, and brave enough to love, and wise enough to know that we have not been left without second chances. Jesus offered those second chances over and over again to those he met:

Zacchaeus was condemned by his community as a greedy tax collector, but Jesus recognized his latent generosity.

The woman at the well who had five husbands: Jesus saw her hunger and thirst for living water. Peter acted like a brave disciple, but Jesus saw a coward's heart. It wasn't much, but Jesus took a risk and believed in him, and Peter became the rock upon which the church was built. In Jesus, God sees what we do not see. There is an invitation to enter paradise again, a Garden in which both the wheat and the weeds are left together, because only God is the harvester. Amen.

Analysis

Matthew's parable was the text for that last Sunday in July. Being a lectionary preacher and a gardener, I selected it to study and preach. My biblical exegesis shed light on Matthew's Jewish adaptation of Mark's Gospel of this same parable. Matthew's parables accent the notion of eschatological judgment as ruled by God's coming kingdom. Scholars debate whether this particular parable (Matthew 13:24–30) was from the Jesus tradition of sayings or from a rabbinical counterpart.[37] I described in the sermon Matthew's frustration with the Christ-followers who were not behaving as he liked, and how therefore Matthew employs judgment to correct their misdeeds. The weeds or evil ones will burn, as in hell. This vehemence of Matthew's arose from his sense of urgency regarding Jesus' imminent return; he felt the church needed to get together — to cooperate. When Jesus did not return, the church itself moved into the role of judge on Earth, determining who belonged and who did not. One way the church determines this is through orthodoxy or right belief, as defined by those in power. In the sermon, I offered several examples of the church operating in this pattern of judge on Earth throughout the centuries so that the congregation to which I was preaching might get a perspective on their own situation.

Rather than literally interpreting Matthew's parable as many have done in the church, I chose to focus on the larger Christian story — a

---

37. William R. Herzog II, *Parables as Subversive Speech* (Louisville: Westminster John Knox Press, 1994), 83.

God of love and life who is always seeking after us. Exegetically I heard Matthew's frustration with human nature and the failure of people to behave in a certain way, the way he wanted. But I also heard God's love and truth as witnessed in Jesus Christ.

Using liberation hermeneutics, I asked what power wheat and weeds had in the congregation. The church has a community garden in the parking lot that contains eight large gardening plots for use by members. There are also several nicely landscaped gardens around the building. The church hires a master gardener to weed and keep the gardens looking attractive. In the Memorial Garden area, volunteers planted perennials and annuals with the agreement to care for them year round. Members take great delight in seeing flowers blooming, desert plants growing, bushes blossoming, and colorful ground cover. Those who plant vegetables in the community garden bring their goods inside to share with others on a weekly basis. As in any human community, there are "weeds" — those who complain that the gardens are not keep up to par, that they are not weeded enough, or that they use too much water. I cannot count how many discussions there have been at staff, budget, and council meetings regarding weeding — its costs and the lack of proper care of the gardens. Knowing that the congregation was conversant in gardening and held a negative view of weeds, I reminded them that weeds are a good force as well and that when composted, weeds make growth possible.

This congregation was in a crisis. They needed to hear a word of hope. Yet that word of hope needed to recognize the evil within. Their ministers had resigned under duress. A congregational vote had invited them back with a slim margin. The senior minister said "no." As their associate minister, I was still in a process of discernment at the time of this sermon. What I knew about them as their pastor and preacher is that for the most part they viewed themselves as wheat among the weeds of the world. They strive to be good, loyal citizens. They take their church duties seriously and faithfully contribute to the budget. If they see weeds or evil cropping up, they are apt to eradicate them as quickly as possible or totally ignore their existence.

In response to the senior minister's coming out, the church did not handle itself well and many people were hurt, specifically the gay and lesbian members of the church. Insensitive comments like, "Will our children be safe now?" and a churchwide survey that identified our sexual orientation as rendering us less capable ministers showed that the congregation was afraid (homophobic) and nervous about its public image of having two gay ministers (heterosexism).

This sermon called members to see each other as God sees us, in all of our weeds and wheat aspects. It did not directly address the ongoing crisis or mention the word "homosexuality." The sermon came as a word of truth in the midst of chaos. It reminded us all of our human condition and the ability to be good and evil. Using parables or speaking symbolically is one way of considering a particular topic or issue without naming it directly. This allows people to hear what they are ready to hear. This is one strategy to assist ministers and congregations with preaching, not only in conflicted settings, but also around difficult topics like sexuality.

Closeted Clergy

There are many LGBT clergy who choose to remain in the closet because church policies do not allow them to be open and also keep their ordination and positions of leadership. By doing this, the church is asking its ministers to lie about a fundamental part of their nature in order to serve God, the God who created them. Lesbians and gay men, bisexual and transgender people have always served God, albeit silently most of the time. With the cultural push in the 1960s and 1970s toward sexual freedom and honesty, eventually the gay community began coming out. Most people mark the Stonewall riots on June 26, 1969, as the beginning of this movement. For almost forty years the church has wandered in the wilderness asking, "What is this (gay and lesbian persons)?" In the wilderness the church is seeking to understand itself in a new paradigm, one that is sexually and scripturally literate. Until then, the LGBT clergy who are out and those who remain in the closet are preaching in ways that shape our future as a church. For those in the closet, the cost is high.

Even so, their faithful preaching delivers God's word even if their sexual identity is unknown or unrevealed. Compare this reality with the truth about biblical texts written by authors whom we do not know, nor do we have a sense of who they are, yet God's word comes to us through their efforts. What follows is a sermon by a closeted lesbian minister who has faithfully served God and her denomination for sixteen years, who won a top prize in preaching, and who regularly illuminates the biblical texts with imagination and Spirit. I include her sermon as a reality check in the church. For a variety of reasons, not every LGBT clergyperson chooses to come out. This particular sermon was preached in a seminary community. It is a persuasive style of preaching, inviting the hearers to answer questions, to repent, to seek, and finally to rejoice.

Sermon:
"LIGHT A LAMP, AND SWEEP, AND SEEK DILIGENTLY"
Anonymous

Texts: Luke 15:8–9; 1 John 4:16–17

"As God is, so are we in this world."

What might it mean for us to be as God is, in this world?

What kind of unmitigated, radical love might we find ourselves caught up in?

What is the charge to us?

What is our responsibility—especially as members of a religious community that claims its center to be the good news of the gospel, but as a matter of course, practices the exclusion and oppression of a whole grouping of God's people? People for whom the church by way of ignoring their presence, silencing their voices, and denying their giftedness as spiritual leaders not only distorts the gospel, but abandons it altogether. Do we in the Christian tradition think that there can be those who have fallen so far from grace that our judgment on them is justified? If we do, then we had better think again.

As the church, will we have compassion and insight enough to know that we have lost one of our precious coins?

Will we have the courage to light a lamp? . . . and will we have a heart bent on justice and mercy and love — enough to sweep and to seek diligently, until we find our lost coin?

If so . . . what rejoicing could be ours!!!

The following is quoted from a letter to the editors of *The Other Side,* an evangelical Christian magazine:

> I don't know why I'm homosexual, nor why neither prayer nor Bible reading, neither psychotherapy nor healing lines have ever "cured" me. I wish I could "come out" openly and share what I know, but the time is too early. . . . I'm tired of seeing the gay bars filled with so many youths who once sincerely accepted Christ as Lord and Savior — only to find they hadn't become heterosexual and so [felt and] feel excluded from the body of Christ. . . . Less than two months ago I was told by a sincere Christian counselor it would be "better" to "repent and die" even if I had to kill myself, than to go on loving and relating to others as a homosexual.

That a letter such as this even exists is hard to believe.

It is probably beyond the ability of most of us to really fathom the betrayal and shame and pain that a precious human being has felt going through the torture of attempt after attempt to become acceptable — just even *acceptable* — at *any* price — to the community professing unconditional love.

The reality that there are those who are kept outside the Body of Christ by those who call themselves Christians, because of the need those Christians have to justify their own compulsory heterosexual expression, is difficult to own.

But all these things as well as the fact that a counselor professing to know something of what the love of Christ is about should
suggest suicide to another human being urgently screams one loud
proclamation to the church and to those of us who participate in the
church—vocal and silent alike.

Friends, WE are in need of repentance and reconciliation.

We need to ask ourselves some hard but basic questions. We
need to take seriously that these questions spring from real lives.
Gay and lesbian people exist. Even if we are unaware of it, they are
members of our families. They are among our friends, our neighbors,
and our brothers and sisters in Christ.

In the book *Is the Homosexual My Neighbor?* the authors pose
some questions to the church (paraphrased):

- Do we care about gays and lesbians gifted for service as dea-
  cons, elders, and ministers who cannot respond to their call
  within the church because the invitation to full participation is
  based on the condition that they must either become straight
  or live celibate lives?

- Does it matter to us that vibrant, faithful men and women
  have been denied ordination in spite of their God-given gifts—
  because of their God-given sexuality?

- Do we care about the pain and injury inflicted upon self-
  confessed gay and lesbian Christians who endure rejection
  from those who make them into scapegoats for their own inner
  alienation?

A pastor told me that three youths from the senior high group
talked with her about being afraid that they were gay. After talking
with them for awhile she told them not to worry, they would probably
"grow out of it." The rest of the topics for the discussions at youth
group that spring were things like "Dating and Mating," "Talking to
the Opposite Sex," "When I Become an Adult and Get Married."

Do we care about hidden gay and lesbian Christians whose self-acceptance is impeded by the well-meaning remarks of those who have not gone to the trouble to understand the oppression of being lesbian or gay living in a heterosexist society?

There are many more questions we might ask, but perhaps the bottom line is, do we care enough about human wholeness to do something constructive about disarming the myths and fears which surround the issue of homosexuality?

The parable of the lost coin has long been one of my favorite parables. It is one of the few images of God as a woman that has nothing to do with God as a parent or as a caregiver. God is not seen in this parable as a mother giving suck to her child, a midwife helping a woman give birth to a child, a mother eagle bearing her nestling on her wing, or as a mother hen gathering her chicks under her wing to protect them. To be sure, these images are rich and beautiful expressions of God's care and love for her children, but the parable of the lost coin presents an interestingly different picture of God.

In this parable it is not the surrounding world that needs God's love and care, but it is God herself who is aware that she needs all ten of her coins and that SHE will have to initiate the search for her lost coin. Nine coins just won't do. All ten coins are important; they are of equal value — if the coins are baubles on a string, then her adornment is incomplete with any coin missing; if the coins are money, then she knows each one is crucial to her budget!!! When she discovers one of the coins is missing, she doesn't wait until morning and she doesn't put out a halfhearted search. She lights her lamp, sweeps with the intention of finding, and seeks diligently until she does find her lost coin.

If it is true that "as God is, so are we in this world," we must light the lamp . . . until we find a way to do justice by working to give voice to our gay, lesbian, bisexual, and transgender brothers and sisters who have been silenced and closeted by our sin and fear . . . for we all have a stake in co-participation, we all have something to say to the church that the church needs for its life.

If we are to be in this world, as God is, we MUST sweep...until we find a way to do justice by recognizing the honorable status of all people, lesbian, gay, bisexual, or straight...no matter what our sexual orientation...as being created good and sexual and as being claimed by God as God's own people.

If we would be in this world, as God is, we must seek diligently ...until we find a way to do justice by becoming the embodiment of God's mercy and love to those we have made and kept outcast, embracing them not as a mother embraces her child, not as one who has superior status condescending to one of lesser status, but as those who know that the co-creative life that we are meant to participate in with God and each other finds its power and motion and beauty and joy in embracing all of God's creation as good, even those we have rejected and kept outcast...even the outcast and rejected aspects of our own selves.

But what might happen if the church were to find herself embracing the outcast? Including the rejected?

"And when she has found the lost coin, she calls together her friends and neighbors, saying, 'Rejoice with me...for I have found the coin which I had lost.'"

It might look like a celebration, friends. It might just look like a celebration.

So let us light a lamp, and sweep, and seek diligently...and we will find each other, and ourselves in all our variegated beauty co-creating with God...and we will ALL rejoice.

Analysis

Exegetically there are two significant insights brought to light in the sermon. In the parable of the woman sweeping for the lost coin, God is likened to this woman, who is neither a mother nor a caregiver — typical images of females — but a woman housekeeper. This housekeeper is not caring for people or the world outside but instead is focused on what she needs. And she needs her ten coins. Rarely in a congregation do we allow the image of God as needing something — whether us or a precious coin — to enter our theological field of vision because we have typically imagined God as all knowing and all powerful. This view of God is problematic especially when it comes to the crucifixion of Jesus. That God "needs" anything is a revolutionary way of viewing this text, perhaps because the preacher knows from her experience as lesbian in the closet of being that lost coin. She makes this point especially clear when she notes that not just anything can replace the lost coin and nine will not do — all are of equal value. Naming the LGBT community as the lost precious coin provides a framework from which to ask the church questions about its responsibility here. Most often it is the LGBT community that is seen as the "problem" and not the churches' loss or responsibility to face.

The other exegetical move that makes this sermon stand out as a biblical model is using the text to ask the question. The author of 1 John describes God as love and then completes the description by saying that those who are like God, do as God does: as God is, so are we in this world. Lifting this description as a challenge to people in the pews brings the text to life in a bold way. No longer can we just sit back and let God be love in the world, we have a responsibility to be love as well. Combining this question with the God who sweeps until she finds the lost coin — the LGBT community — invites the church to repent of exclusion and begin being like God is, full of love for all people. The sermon ends on a high point of celebration when the coin is found, when the LGBT people are recognized within the church.

Conclusion

In both of these sermons the experience as lesbian women informed our interpretation of the biblical texts as preachers. This illustrates the hermeneutical task at hand in writing and preaching sermons — we bring our lives and faithful service into conversation with the biblical tradition. Reclaiming the Bible for lesbian and gay people means we have an interpretation that reflects the realities of our lives as lived invisibly and visibly on the margin. In the case of these two sermons, because I was already out as a lesbian, I did not need to specifically address the negative judgment (heterosexism) by some about lesbian and gay clergy. On the other hand, the closeted lesbian preacher chose to directly address the oppression and insidious behavior toward LGBT people by some people. Her position in the closet did not limit the ability to speak a Word about God's nature as one of love and the worth of all of God's people, including lesbians and gay men. As an out lesbian preacher, my presence in the pulpit spoke loud and clear on this relationship. I chose to remove the words "lesbian" and "gay," "homophobic" or "heterosexist" from the sermon and instead talk about the ways in which we all judge each other. In the end, the theological message is the same, but the homiletical methods differ.

The Bible is central to a lesbian and gay homiletic; marked by a passion for justice, both truth telling and speaking on behalf of those who are marginalized. Esther's story is one biblical model of what it might mean for LGBT people to come out and claim full humanity and opportunity within the Christian tradition. Esther's story also includes those who need to remain in the closet (hidden), but whose preaching can still be effective. Exegetically, the story also invites straight allies to speak on behalf of their lesbian sisters and gay brothers, knowing that there is risk involved. However, we have not done this alone. The inclusion of out gay and lesbian Christians in the church has come about through the faithful and loving preaching of heterosexuals. Their willingness to come out has helped to pave the way for full inclusion, including ordination in some churches. Proclamation of the gospel includes the welcome of all God's creation; many straight and closeted clergy have given powerful witness in their sermons. These and LGBT preachers will reclaim the Bible for powerful and prophetic preaching.

Chapter 4

Theology Comes Out

Through books, articles, journals, sermons, lectures, magazines, and videos, the voices of LGBT Christians have become a choir with a wide vocal range. As more theological and biblical work is produced by lesbian, gay, bisexual, and transgender Christians, a distinctive collection of theology has emerged. Recent titles give a good indication of the variety: *Queering Christ* (Robert E. Goss), *Queer Commentary and the Hebrew Bible* (Ken Stone), *The Queer God* (Marcella Althaus-Reid), *The Man Jesus Loved: Homoerotic Narrative from the New Testament* (Theodore W. Jennings Jr.), and *Gay Perspective: Things Our Homosexuality Tells Us about the Nature of God and the Universe* (Edwin C. Johnson and Toby Johnson). The current president of Metropolitan Community Churches (MCC), Rev. Dr. Nancy Wilson, authored a book, *Our Tribe*, whose chapter titles give a clear indication to which tribe she is referring: "A Queer Theology of Sexuality," "Outing the Bible: Our Gay and Lesbian Tribal Texts," and "Outing the Sodomite," all evidence of the intersection of gay and lesbian perspectives of Christianity.[1] Writing about LGBT theologies is difficult since its growth is so rapid that ideas develop more quickly than the ink dries on paper. The good news is, we actually have historical material to critique. We have a collective voice that is not of one mind, but all the same is singing, constantly creating new music.

Coming out theologically, for the most part, has meant seeking inclusion in the church, finding room at the table, and wanting the same privileges of membership as other Christians, specifically ordination.

---

1. Nancy Wilson, *Our Tribe: Queer Folks, God, Jesus, and the Bible* (San Francisco: HarperCollins, 1995), contents page.

While substantial in content and critical of traditional Christianity, LGBT theology produced in the last few decades fought for recognition, identity, and empowerment. This path, while initially necessary, has its limitations, as feminist Catholic theologian Mary E. Hunt notes: "Despite the scholarly production, the primary discourse among church people on matters of same-sex love in the early twenty-first-century continues to be based on the normative character of male sexual experience, male religious experience, and male models of power."[2] There is more theological work to be done besides just cleaning out our closets. We in the homiletical and theological field need to bring our resources to bear not only on the coming out process but also on the class, race, gender, and accessibility concerns that narrate our human condition.

Even so, these resources, radical in title and nature, bring LGBT voices into the ongoing theological conversation within Christianity. They ask and then respond to the essential questions theologians have asked throughout history, "How do I know God?" "Who is God for me?" "How is the biblical story about God authentic to my experience of God?" "Where am I in the story?" "Who is Christ for me?" For preachers, the questions take on the added dimension of how we communicate these findings to others. What is our methodology? What are our theological underpinnings as we write and preach sermons? Specifically, how do we create and preach sermons so that the biblical word of God becomes flesh among us in our preaching?

One of the major tasks of a lesbian and gay homiletic is to incorporate and extend these new theological insights into preaching. As a sexual minority in society and the church, LGBT people are faced with the task of integrating sexuality and theology in ways unlike any other community. Sermons about sexuality are rare, and until recently little attention was given to our sexual experience in relation

---

2. Mary E. Hunt, "Queering Old Time Religion," *Literature and Theology: An International Journal of Religion, Theory and Culture* 15, no. 3 (September 2001): 213.

to God. In fact, a study done of fifty sermons preached in LGBT-majority-populated churches (Protestant and Roman Catholic), where one would be more likely to hear about sexuality, discovered that rarely do preachers mention sex, sexuality, or relationships.[3] But, because many LGBT Christians have been willing to come out and speak about their lives with honesty and integrity, the level of dialogue has gone from shame to a modified understanding of the need to talk about sexuality. This conversation about sexuality is intended to be freeing for heterosexuals too. The gifts that out lesbian women, gay men, bisexuals, and transgender Christians bring to theological conversation are meant for the liberation and salvation of all, not just ourselves. In this work, however, we find ways to speak theologically about sexuality in our sermons and in our lives.

Historical View of Lesbian, Gay, and Queer Theology

Before delving into particular theological concepts from a gay and lesbian perspective, we should note that there is not a single gay or lesbian theology.[4] In the brief forty years of out lesbian and gay ministers, various theologies have developed in relation to the need, context, and author's own theological bias. Prior to this time religious books about lesbians and gay men were written primarily by straight psychologists, medical doctors, and theologians in the "research and study" period.[5] Their interest was educational — primarily for biblical study and policy development in churches, but from a straight perspective. However, lesbian and gay theology has not emerged in a

---

3. Mark B. Lee, "Hearing the Eunuch's Children: Preaching in Gay, Lesbian, Bisexual and Transgender Communities," D.Min project (Iliff School of Theology, 2006), 22.

4. While bisexual and transgender theological discourse is available and growing, I am concentrating specifically on same-sex love.

5. Theological studies by the Presbyterians, Methodists, Roman Catholics, Lutherans, Episcopalians, Baptists, Unitarians, and Disciples of Christ...as early as 1965.

vacuum or apart from the second half of the twentieth-century's theology. Therefore, it generally follows liberal theological development that we have witnessed since the mid-twentieth century in the United States.

Finding themselves at odds with their local churches and denominations, lesbian and gay Christians reacted by finding their voices through liberal theology, liberation theology, and feminist theology. Using each one of these developments to argue for the inclusion and affirmation of same-sex love, lesbians, gay men, and our allies began writing and speaking out against rejection and condemnation from most Christian denominations. Over time and with experience, lesbians, gay men, and our allies have carved out a grounded theology pertaining to same-sex love.

Through the "research and study" period, many denominations formed committees to report to authorizing bodies regarding policy toward same-sex love. In the Presbyterian Church (USA), year after year of General Assembly studies finally culminated in a 1991 report called "Keeping Body and Soul Together: Sexuality, Spirituality, and Social Justice." The report gave an extensive theological introduction regarding sexuality in American culture in the late 1980s, as its work spanned at least four years. The published report sold more than a hundred thousand copies, but was ultimately rejected by the General Assembly for fear that any positive word about lesbians and gay men (which was only a small portion of the total report) would split the denomination.[6] What emerged though has remained and is theologically significant — it held "justice-love" as the defining mark of an intimate relationship between two people. In this report, mutuality and respect, rather than literal interpretations of Scripture, were the sought-after hallmarks of sexual behavior. These hallmarks of justice-love were derived from scriptural mandates of justice and love that originate in and are fed by God. *Keeping Body and Soul Together* was

---

6. Marvin M. Ellison and Sylvia Thorson-Smith, eds., *Body and Soul: Rethinking Sexuality as Justice-Love* (Cleveland: Pilgrim Press, 2003), 5–14.

unapologetically liberationist, feminist, and sex-positive; it has come to be highly regarded as a groundbreaking report that has paved the way for others to continue thinking about God and sex.

Another endeavor toward a "theology of its own" is queer theology. It began in mid-1990 as queer theory intersected with theologians in the lesbian and gay community. One definition of queer theory is "a postmodern philosophy that dismisses 'identity' as too fixed a notion for the fluidity, change, and 'transgressive boundaries' that are the stuff of real life."[7] Queer theology has been taught by Dr. Carter Heyward at Episcopal Divinity School at Harvard since 1995. Her definition of "queer" is broad; it includes LGBT persons, but also the larger movement on behalf of such persons, the theoretical post-modern movement, and last, but not least, any group or persons who are publicly in solidarity with lesbian, gay, bisexual, and transgender people.[8] One specific contribution Heyward has made to lesbian and gay theology, and now queer theology, is equating sacred power with sexual energy. Most studies about sexuality have God and sex neatly separated, whereas Heyward believes our erotic power is the same life force that we call God.[9] This bringing together of sexuality and spirituality is key in developing a queer theology.

Anglican priest and English theologian Elizabeth Stuart offers a comprehensive historical look at the emergence of lesbian and gay theology and then critiques it in light of her theological understanding of Christianity. Her book *Gay and Lesbian Theologies: Repetitions with Critical Difference* begins with a short review of theologies that have emerged in the last century. Stuart describes liberal theology as a reflection on the meaning of human experience and Christian faith, articulated by primarily European American white males like Paul Tillich, H. Richard Niebuhr, Martin Buber, and Rudolf Bultmann.

---

7. Ibid., 86.
8. Ibid., 88.
9. Carter Heyward, *Touching Our Strength: The Erotic as Power and the Love of God* (San Francisco: Harper & Row, 1989).

Existential human experience, especially World War II, influenced liberal theology as theologians struggled to make sense of human evil and
suffering. In response to liberal theology, neo-orthodoxy emerged as a
corrective and placed the emphasis on the radical difference between
God and humanity. One leader of this movement, Swiss theologian
Karl Barth, wrote in defense of neo-orthodoxy, "Let God be God
and man be man."[10] Barth stressed that God could not be located
in "man's" choices because God was far above the powers of humanity. That God in Christ had suffered and died for humanity was the
core message of neo-orthodoxy. This message was received well by
those in middle- to upper-strata churches with access to resources,
power, and pleasure. However, this message did not, in fullness, sat-
isfy those in lower income brackets, rural areas, the urban streets,
the barrios, and underdeveloped sectors of society who wanted God
to do something for their situation. Studying Scripture and asking
about God from these margins created a different sort of theology.
People of faith in these places discovered a liberating God who is with
people in suffering to bring new life. The God of liberation ultimately
wants justice for all people. Liberation theology, which locates God
in the conflicts between human beings, expects social transformation.
Women, blacks, immigrants, and poor people studied the Bible and
clearly found God on their side. Early Latin American liberation theologians such as Leonardo Boff, Gustavo Gutiérrez, and Jon Sobrino
stressed that liberation theology is concerned with systems of social
injustice that cause the sufferings of people.[11] U.S. theologian Robert
McAfee Brown wrote extensively on liberation theology, bringing it
to awareness within mainline denominations.[12] Liberation theology

---

10. Karl Barth, *The Humanity of God* (Richmond, VA: John Knox Press, 1960),
42.

11. Leonardo Boff, *Way of the Cross — Way of Justice* (Maryknoll, NY: Orbis Books,
1980); Gustavo Gutiérrez, *A Theology of Liberation: History Politics, and Salvation*
(Maryknoll, NY: Orbis Books, 1972); Jon Sobrino, *Jesus in Latin America* (Maryknoll,
NY: Orbis Books, 1987).

12. Robert McAfee Brown, *Spirituality and Liberation: Overcoming the Great Fallacy* (Philadelphia: Westminster Press, 1988); *Liberation Theology: An Introductory*

spread like wildfire among indigenous populations and in numerous contexts other than Latin America, such as South Africa and Asia.

The next shift in theological development in the second half of the twentieth century intersects with the postmodern condition in which we find ourselves and our world. While liberal and liberation theologies are more familiar, postmodern theology is newer and not as widely discussed. Postmodern theory and theology will not be defined definitively, for that is part of the definition of postmodernism — that there is not a definite point to most anything, including a definition. Yet, for the purposes of historical inquiry, Stuart describes postmodern theology as the reclaiming of the text, biblical and otherwise. She claims that postmodern theology is a response to the end of metanarrative.[13] The modern era has ended, and with its end has come a collapse of truth, self, and God. Stuart writes, "These theologians declare that there is no secular realm, no space beyond divine elucidation...no dualism between faith and reason or grace and nature."[14]

Stuart uses these theological lenses to categorize theologies written by, about, and from the lesbian and gay perspective. With the exception of neo-orthodoxy, each theology is applied to the gay and lesbian movement and studies. In the end, Stuart announces that each of these is bankrupt. Lesbian and gay theology, she writes, has failed to address real human issues like the AIDS crisis, which brought many theological questions of death, heaven, and resurrection. The primary focus has been the oppression of gay and lesbian people within the Christian church and the need for inclusion. Liberal, liberationist,

---

Guide (Louisville: Westminster John Knox Press, 1993); and *Speaking of Christianity* (Louisville: Westminster John Knox Press, 1997).

13. A metanarrative can include any grand, all-encompassing story, classic text, or archetypal account of the historical record. It can also provide a framework upon which an individual's own experiences and thoughts may be ordered. These grand, all-encompassing stories are typically characterized by some form of "transcendent and universal truth" in addition to an evolutionary tale of human existence (a story with a beginning, middle, and end). See Wikipedia, s.v. "metanarrative," *www://en.wikipedia.org/wiki/Metanarrative*.

14. Elizabeth Stuart, *Gay and Lesbian Theologies: Repetitions with Critical Difference* (England: Ashgate Publishing Limited, 2003), 6.

and feminist theologies by lesbian and gay authors, Stuart writes, have failed to address the crisis of death created by AIDS.

In response to this failure, Stuart points to queer theology as a recent and radically different theology (postmodern). The difference between the two is that queer theology is interested in liberation from contemporary constructions of gender and sexuality. Thus, the rallying cry is not "Come Out," but "What is a sexual identity and who needs it?" In summary, Stuart claims that Christianity, in and of itself, is "queer" and that sexual identities have no ultimate significance. One dictionary defines "queer" as "deviating from the expected or normal; strange; odd or unconventional in behavior; eccentric; *slang* Homosexual."[15] Here, Stuart is using the dual meaning of the word "queer" to further distinguish her theology from traditional gay and lesbian theology. As Christians who also identify as lesbians or as gay men, we are queer both in the sense of being odd and being homosexual.

Stuart locates queer theology squarely within the church by using both Protestant sacraments, baptism and Eucharist, as a theological springboard. In baptism she locates Christian identity with the new creation in Christ, by which we have died and risen to a new being. This is the "queer" thing — that in our culture not all people are baptized Christians, and yet Christians are called to live in a specific way that sets them apart from general society. One wonders if Stuart is suggesting a secular versus Christian society. Our Christian identity through baptism is given to us by God and is nonnegotiable. Therefore, the baptized belong to another world (queer-odd or strange), regardless of whether they are gay or straight. Stuart explains the Eucharist as the new covenant through which a new reality is opened up that creates a new community — the body of Christ to which we all belong — gay and straight, bisexual and transgender, queer and questioning. The Eucharist is also the place where we rehearse the life to come, the communion of saints, and dwell in the mystical union with

---

15. William Morris, ed., *The American Heritage Dictionary of the English Language* (Boston: Houghton Mifflin, 1980), 1070.

those departed. The body of Christ that is shared in the Eucharist is the body of the baptized — the church — who are redirected to worship God and proclaim the gospel. So, she concludes:

> Since gender and sexual identification have no ultimate signifi-
> cance in Christian theology, marriage cannot be understood as
> a heterosexual institution any more than monasticism can be-
> cause heterosexuality does not "really" (that is, eschatologically)
> exist. Those who, in the cultural construction of our day, are
> labeled lesbian and gay are entitled to the same paths of holi-
> ness as everyone else and all are entitled to have the path of
> monasticism recommended. . . . [16]

Stuart's queer theology has yet to reach most mainline Protestant churches. Her insights regarding lesbian and gay theology might un-lock the current impasse within denominations. As Stuart's vision for lesbian and gay (queer) persons and the (queer) Christian faith find their way into American pulpits, the response will be noteworthy.

Moving from this broad sketch of lesbian, gay, and queer theol-ogy to specific theological concepts, the first thing to note is that there is no way to include all or even most of them in this work. However, there are three significant theological concepts meaning-ful to the LGBT community: *creation, incarnation,* and *resurrection.* Rather than being understood as abstract theological constructs, each of these deals with the "body" or physical world: the earth body, the human body, and the heavenly body or resurrection. In the lesbian, gay, bisexual, and transgender world, since our difference is in sexual expression and gender identity, our bodies are therefore of particular importance in reflecting on God. Christianity claims that we are all made in the image of God. Thus, creation is central to both the ori-gins of Christianity and our self-understanding of being created in the image of God. What follows is a reflection on creation from lesbian

---

16. Stuart, *Gay and Lesbian Theologies,* 113.

and gay men within the Christian community. The theological concepts of incarnation and resurrection will be illustrated through two sermons. Studying theological concepts from sermons gives a window into our theology. Both sermons are by out gay clergy, but at the time of preaching one of them was still closeted.

Creation, In the Image of God

One of our primary tasks in understanding same-sex love is listening to lesbians and gay men talk about how they understand themselves to be made in the image of God. Iliff School of Theology professor and UCC minister Dr. Larry Kent Graham's book *Discovering Images of God: Narratives of Care among Lesbians and Gays* is based on a series of extensive interviews with lesbian and gay Christians. In a desire to understand the spirituality and spiritual lives of lesbian and gay men, Graham listened to their stories about Christian formation and identification. As we listen to the lives of lesbian women, gay men, bisexuals, and transgender people speak about God, what emerges is a picture of a creative Creator. In the last two chapters, Graham constructs a theology of "Imago Dei," the image of God, in response to the interviews. In one of the narratives, a gay man asks, "Why do we honor diversity of nature in God's creation, but not the diversity of people in God's creation?"[17] This is a good question. It is the fundamental theological argument about homosexuality. Some argue, "We are born this way" — an essentialist view, versus, "It's a choice we make" — a social constructionist view. The former suggests that we cannot help being gay because it is the way we were born, which can put same-sex people in the victim role. The latter suggests we have a choice in the matter, and are intentionally sinful if sexually active. Those who call "it" (homosexuality/same-sex love) a sin have not seen us as people created in the image of God. For lack of better understanding, they have tried to separate the sin from the sinner, as

---

17. Larry Graham, *Discovering Images of God: Narratives of Care among Lesbians and Gays* (Louisville: Westminster John Knox Press, 1997), 57.

in the misguided aphorism, "Hate the sin, and love the sinner." With sin considered an action rather than a state of being, it is easier to separate the person from the sin. When Christians denigrate same-sex love, Episcopal bishop and gay priest Gene Robinson counters, "What most people don't realize is that homosexuality is something I am, it's not something that I do. It's at the very core of who I am. We're not talking about taking a liberal or conservative stance on a particular issue; we're talking about who I am."[18] A holistic look at creation, with each person created in the image of God, does not allow separation. What we "do" or how we express our being sexually cannot then be called a sin for some and not others. If that is so, then acting on one's heterosexual desires would be a sin as well.

That human beings are made in the image of God originates in Genesis, where we find two distinct creation stories. In the first, male and female together form the image of God. In the second creation story, humanity is made from the earth — the earthlings are without a particular gender until Adam (*H'adam* — of the earth) gets lonely and wants a companion, and Eve (Ish-feminine in Hebrew) the female is created from his rib or side. Neither refers specifically to sexual identity or orientation, nor does it explain what it means to be female and male. The Christian church has interpreted first and second Genesis in strictly heterosexual terms, meaning that male and female must marry and reproduce in order to reflect the goodness of God's creation. This interpretation has provided a certain stability within society and nations. When Genesis was written, the Hebrew people were making sense of gender: where did male and female come from and how did the differences work? The presence of same-sex love, bisexuality, and transgender (moving from one gender to another) has disrupted this stability, and this is what is so frightening to many Christians and threatens to split denominations. Would that we could step back from the binary divisions of male/female, gay/straight, black/white, and see

---

18. Gene Robinson, "A Church Asunder," *The New Yorker*, April 17, 2006, 58.

our common humanity for what it is: all of us made in the image of God. All are precious in God's creation.

Sex and God

Perhaps if church leaders explained sexual expression as part of God's creation, a gift rather than a sin, understanding would be greater among laity. The purpose of sexual practice is not just reproduction, but a means through which we experience the love of God. By loving another person we are drawn into the mystery of divine love here on earth. Heterosexual desire is not the ultimate goal of sexual intercourse; rather, it is the desire of God that we seek through our bodily interaction. Interestingly enough, when the Apostle Paul is trying to describe to the Corinthians the bodily resurrection, he goes into a lengthy discourse on human, cosmic, and divine bodies. In his explanation, Paul uses the cosmos as an example of diversity, "There is one glory of the sun, and another glory of the moon, and another glory of the stars; indeed star differs from star in glory" (1 Corinthians 15:41). Why, then, is sexual expression not seen in light of the diversity of creation? Even the stars are different from one another, but they are all stars. Gay, lesbian, bisexual, and transgender people are different, but we are all human beings, no better, no worse than our heterosexual counterparts. This argument plays into Stuart's theological point that as Christians we are all welcome at the table and sexual identity is not relevant.

It would be great if this were the case. However, many gay men and lesbian women's experience of coming out in the church is fraught with tension and inhospitality. In my experience of being a colleague to a senior minister coming out to his congregation, I witnessed up close one congregation's response, which was tragically human and ended in his resignation. Over time, I have wondered what his coming out publicly to the congregation did to their understanding of God. He was a straight man, or so they had thought, married, and with children, which reinforced the heterosexual values and standards by which the congregation ordered their lives. From the beginnings of this church (and most other churches), the congregation's understanding of God was shaped by pastoral leadership with senior ministers as heterosexual, married men with families. No doubt our image of God develops in a myriad of ways — though the preacher/minister is one of the strongest influences for those who find their spiritual life in the church. One might say that with this example of a spiritual life we are relying on heterosexuality and reproduction of children — the traditional family — as a means of salvation. In a sense, Christians have elevated heterosexual males to a place of worship, thus Mary Daly's contention that "If God is male, then male is God." Likewise we could say, "If God is straight, then straight is God." This could become a trap of idolatry. When what once worked and seemed to be fitting becomes too comfortable, then it becomes our security blanket. Anyone who changes the order is accused of destroying "God" (the holy). Remember the Golden Calf incident in the desert with Moses (Exodus) and the term "sacred cows" as used by church consultant William Easum.[19] Both are examples of how people organize around certain ideas and beliefs to manage the chaos of life. But when those practices become the "God" or "the Holy," then we are not free to hear God in the still small voice or meet the stranger, who is Christ.

If a straight married male minister is all the congregation has known as a spiritual leader, and if suddenly this supposedly heterosexual minister comes out as a gay man, it is not surprising that the congregation's understanding of God would be affected. The experience challenges our views and ideas of the Divine. Before their eyes their image of God went from straight to gay — or has masqueraded as such. This fluidity and change is what postmodern theory aims to address — that life is truly in flux, that no sexual orientation is stable, and that our idolatrous images of God will collapse. When Jesus comes and is proclaimed to be the Messiah, there are a great many who are disappointed that

19. William M. Easum, *Sacred Cows Make Gourmet Burgers: Ministry Anytime, Anywhere by Anyone* (Nashville: Abingdon Press, 1995).

he did not rule as they had expected a Messiah would. Jesus did not fit the description they had for One who is of God. Yet every time one of our expectations or idols is exposed, we have the opportunity to be drawn deeper into the mysteries of God.[20] Postmodern theology or queer theology brings together the diverse expressions of sexuality and gender, while concentrating the focus on God. So our challenge is to imagine a church as a queer community, proud of their integration of sexuality and spirituality, and holding fast to that ever-elusive God.

Incarnation

Intricately linked to creation is incarnation. God as the author of creation created the heavens and the earth and all that dwells therein; God's embodiment in Jesus is reflected in the gospel: the Word made flesh in Jesus and the continual presence of Christ in and through the church's witness. We are familiar with the expression: "We are God's hands in the world." Bringing the divine Spirit into a material realm that can be touched, seen, and felt is crucial to the gospel of Christianity. But this has not been easy. The belief that the Divine has entered into the human situation, specifically in Jesus, to transform humanity was not fully embraced, even by the disciples. In dealing with the earthly humanity of Jesus, God's son — the holy one, pure and sinless — we very often fail to acknowledge the body as the realm of God, and hence our bodies as dwelling places of the divine. While we have no trouble celebrating the birth of Jesus as a baby, often we stop there and miss his humanity as an adult. God also chose to dwell in humanity, not only in a temple or on a mountaintop, or in a cloud. Author and theologian James Nelson attempts to reconcile the body and sexuality with Christianity, when he writes, "We long for the time when human sexuality, in spite of all its ambiguities, will be more integrated with our experience of the sacred and with the vision

---

20. Barbara Brown Taylor, *God in Pain: Teaching Sermons on Suffering* (Nashville: Abingdon Press, 1998), 20.

of God's shalom."[21] Rather than beginning with Scripture to tell us about our bodies, Nelson advances a "body theology" that begins with the body and its experience before turning to God, the church, or Scripture. Beginning with the body as a location of our experience of the sacred or God, we interpret and give theological meaning to our bodily life. Through awareness of our personal body we move outward to examining our connections to other bodies, our connection to the earth body, and the Christian body within the church. Depending on the interpretive mode in which we view these bodily experiences, we arrive at meaning that feeds our theological understanding of the role sexual expression has within Christian practice. And of course this varies considerably. From a transgender point of view, the body has its own challenges that are different from those of sexual minorities. Rev. Justin Tanis, a transgendered preacher, writes:

> We (trans community) must remember that the struggle around trans bodies is not with those bodies per se, but with the meaning attached to them by society, by medical science, by our lovers, and by our families.... We need to take a holistic look at trans lives and shake off the self-hate that traps many of us in ways more complex and nefarious than simply being in the "wrong" body.[22]

In addition, a study of the relationship between theology and the body opens up new theological paths in which we can explore more fully the incarnation.

LGBT Discoveries

Those who have discovered their sexual expression to be other than heterosexual (the expected norm) have had to take a journey into

---

21. James B. Nelson, *Body Theology* (Louisville: Westminster John Knox Press, 1992), 16.
22. Justin Tanis, *Trans-gendered: Theology, Ministry, and Communities of Faith* (Cleveland: Pilgrim Press, 2003), 162.

the body to learn why heterosexuality did not work for us. For trans-gendered persons, their learning takes place in the body as well. This work among LGBT Christians is healing the split between sexual-ity and spirituality and between genders. Christian history and life have not been affirming of the body in general, much less the sexual or sensual desires of humanity. Professor and sexual theologian Lisa Isherwood describes our awakening like this:

> While the majority of Christians still believe that God sets out the dos and don'ts connected with the body there are others who are waking up to the fact that Christian bodies like other bodies have very little that is "essential" but they have been constructed and set on a treadmill that serves worldly powers.[23]

Listening to what our bodies tell us rather than what society tells us is a major cultural shift. During these changing times, it will seem chaotic as we discover and recover what it means to be human and holy together. With his transgender experience reminding us of the common human experience, Tanis writes that "the queer Christ is shocking to some and liberating to others, and, at best, we can allow ourselves to be both shocked and freed, to be challenged and to be conformed, to be human and holy."[24] Realizing that our bodies are the container in which we live and move and have our being in this physical world, it follows that our holiness is also contained within our bodies. This awareness that our physical space is significant in relation to self, Spirit, and another expands our understanding of the Incarnation. It is common knowledge that we need to be touched in order to survive, that human life is dependent upon positive and loving physical touch. "Body theology" makes great sense for a whole community of people within our churches. The body's wisdom can

---

23. Lisa Isherwood, "Queering Christ: Outrageous Acts and Theological Rebel-lions," *Literature and Theology* 15, no. 3 (September 2001): 250.

24. Tanis, *Trans-gendered*, 142.

lead us to deeper connection to God within, a deeper truth about ourselves as well as others.

≈

The sermon that follows illustrates the power of discovering one's truth through the bodily experience of dancing. Prior to his coming out publicly as a gay man, Rev. Landis preached the following:

Sermon:
"WHEN SOMEONE OPENS THE DOOR"
by Scott Landis

Text: Luke 4:21–30

Several months ago, the church council commissioned a group of people in our congregation to form what we have called the vision team. The work of that group has been to dissect our church's mission statement line by line, to describe it in different ways using a variety of words, as well as biblical images in order to understand fully the values that underlie it. The goal is that members of this team will help the various ministries and fellowship groups do their work in making decisions and creating new programs for our church.

The word-smithing work has, at times, become quite tedious. But something quite unexpected and remarkable has happened. Our facilitator asked each of us, on a preassigned night, to share our faith story, our spiritual journey in any way we chose with the group. That practice has proven to be transformative as we have begun to see the one sharing his or her journey in a completely new light. What we have experienced externally begins to take on depth and greater meaning as their story is spoken. I have a much better understanding of how God has and continues to work in the lives of each one who has shared their truth, and told their stories more so than I have ever known before. When someone opens the door and reveals previously unknown parts of her or his life, a bond is created, intimacy experienced, and the possibility of community unfolds.

Women tend to be better at this than men, but every now and then even men catch a glimpse of this. The other evening, at the men's gourmet dinner we honored WWII veterans. It was quite remarkable really. These men, some of whom have not spoken about their experiences in years, freely shared some of the joys and pain of those difficult years in their lives. Those of us who listened, who haven't a clue of the intensity of their emotion, were changed a bit as someone opened the door to us and we were invited to enter a world that may be foreign to us.

I meet biweekly with a group of area senior ministers from different denominations. These men and women each have difficult jobs managing large churches with multiposition staffs and smaller than necessary budgets, and all pressures that go with shepherding a nonprofit volunteer organization. Yet as the truth is told, when someone opens the door to their lives by sharing faith stories and deep personal concerns, an amazing bond occurs. For the moment, I am no longer Dr. or Rev. Landis. I am Scott. I am me.

Have you ever been involved in a group like that? If you have, you know exactly what I am talking about. One in which we get away from talking about all we have done or are doing. One in which we allow others to break through our patina, our façade of having it all together, and we open the door to our truest self that others might see us for who we are, and possibly not what they expect.

I recently rediscovered how vital this is to our own sense of integrity in an amazing and beautiful film I have now seen two times and most likely will go to see again. It's a story of a little boy who at age eleven is probably more mature than most adults. Raised in a small mining town in northeast England, Billy is supposed to do what boys do — at least according to his father's way of thinking. His dad, despite the financial hardship of being on strike, gives him fifty pence each week for boxing lessons. However, Billy, intrigued by the ballet class going on in the same hall, eventually gravitates to that side of the gym and there discovers his passion.

In dance, he connects with his soul. Through dance, he flies like a bird, which somehow takes him outside of himself. His dance, he describes, is like electricity, it pulses through his body without beginning or end. Through the dance, he opens the door and allows people to see his truth, this being, his self. However, his dad, so afraid of what this might mean or what others might say, absolutely forbids him to dance.

That could be the end of the story. Billy could have allowed the strength of his father, a white-hot anger demonstrated in both physical and verbal abuse, and the fear that he could get himself killed squelch his passion. He could have donned the boxing gloves once again and do what all good boys from Durham do. Most of us take the route out of fear. For all speak well of us when we do what is expected, do they not?

Remember, Jesus was on a roll. Expecting he would do for those in Nazareth what he did in Capernaum, they wanted to hear a nice sermon that they could compliment him on as they shook his hand at the door. Instead, he opened the door to truth, a truth in this instance that was difficult to hear because it exposed their desire to keep outsiders where they thought they belonged. In holding up truth, through words from their own Hebrew text, Jesus revealed to them who he was — one who came to preach good news to the poor, release the captives, give recovery of sight to the blind, let the oppressed go free, and proclaim the acceptable year of the Lord. Jesus reminded them, "Today this scripture is fulfilled in your hearing."

When someone opens the door, when truth is revealed, when we share our heart, then there is no turning back. In so doing, we discover our true self — beautifully and wonderfully made. We can neither deny it, nor act like it doesn't exist. We can only honor it, thank God for it, and allow it to be. This can be dangerous territory. There may be consequences for such a risk. Remember how quickly the crowd changed their minds about him?

They drove him out of town, and led him to the brow of the hill on which the town was built, so that they might hurl him off the cliff. But he passed through the midst of them and went on his way. As Jesus did that, he forced the crowd to confront their own truth. That was their responsibility — not the responsibility of the one who opens the door.

Billy's mother died when he was a very young child. His memories of her were vague, built around fantasy and answers to his questions about her. The one tangible thing he had from her was a letter. Written in the form of an apology, she asks forgiveness for not being with him physically throughout his life. She tells of how proud she is of him and is grateful for the privilege of having him as her child. Having read this letter thousands of times, Billy recites the letter as his dance instructor reads it. Her last line is both a challenge and a gift when she says, "Always, be yourself."

It was those words that give Billy Elliot the courage to stand up for himself, to his father, to the backwards community in which he lived and danced — to honor his truth no matter what might come. When someone does that, when someone opens the door to his or her soul, some amazing things can happen — not just to that individual, but to all those around — those with ears to hear and eyes to see — those who are attentive.

You see, as we honor our truth, by being our self — and as we articulate that truth in our dance, in our song, in our words, in our deeds — we give others the permission to do the same, and real truth prevails. We are set free!

The moment of truth came for Billy one night when his father caught him in the gym showing his friend a dance. His father was so furious that he could barely contain himself. After an interminable period of staring between the two — a deafening silence — Billy stamps his foot and breaks into his dance. It is his dance of truth. It is his dance of self. It is his way of saying to his father, "This is who I am. I can neither deny it nor act like it doesn't exist. I can only honor it and allow it to be me." It's wonderful. It's so powerful. It's exhilarating, but it can be risky — for we don't know where it will go. But as we take that risk we open the door to the possibility that others will own their truth as well.

As Billy takes that very risky step of accepting and expressing his truth, he invites his father also to be liberated — to become truly who he is.

The truth, my friends, has a remarkable way with us. When I allow the door to open and speak my truth, when I take a risk, I invite you to do likewise. And as I tell my part of the story and you listen, and as you tell your part of the story and I listen, we create the possibility of wholeness. "For I know in part, and you know in part, but when the perfect comes that which is partial will pass away." In the meantime, we're all we have.

In my first parish, I worked with a senior minister whom I admired and respected. I learned much from this man who became a mentor. He allowed me to try new things, but was always there to pick up the pieces when I failed. He encouraged me and gave me hope that one day I might do the same kind of work he did. The problem, however, was that I never knew him. So good at hiding his emotions, feelings, passions, and dreams I never really knew him. We experienced a great deal together and had a terrific working relationship, but there was always something that separated us.

It was not until the day I informed him that I was taking a new position that he broke down and wept. I had never seen him do that before. This spiritual giant was crumbling before me. I felt guilty. I felt responsible but didn't know how to respond.

Not long thereafter, I felt a sense of anger. I had been cheated from ever really knowing this man whom I had cared so much for and who deeply cared for me.

Friends, as we come together in this community we call church, we have got to realize that life is too short for this level of superficiality. If the Spirit of the Lord is truly upon us we must recognize it as a spirit of truth. One that opens the doors to our souls so that our eyes are opened and we truly see. I don't want to get to the end of my journey with only the assurance that I performed well. That all thought well of me.

No, I want to dance! I want to take the risk to honor my truth — to be fully the one whom God created which may just open the possibility of you doing the same. I believe if we do this, we will know love. We will know truth. We will know peace. We will be free!

Analysis

Reading it now, some might see where Landis was in his own coming out process when he admits he wants to risk honoring his truth. The sermon also invites the hearers to listen to their truth and be who they really are. This sermon certainly affirms the saying that "Preachers preach what they most need to hear." It has a bittersweet poignancy as Landis was internally wrestling with what it might be like for him to speak his truth, even to himself at that point. The movie, *Billy Elliot*, to which he refers gave him courage to move forward in his spiritual journey. At that time, though, very few of us really understood his story behind this sermon, but it was a beginning of realizing that Landis was heading into a deeper reality about truth telling. Much later, after he came out to the congregation, we realized he had struggled with his sexual orientation in the closet, but right in front of us.

An exploration of what "truth" and Truth stand for, as related to the Gospels and particularly the story in Luke of Jesus speaking his truth, would help hearers make connections to their own lives. Since Landis does not reveal any particular truth about himself in this sermon, it leaves it open for the listener to determine what that might mean. This is similar to the sermon "Wheat and Weeds" (chapter 3), because he does not name his sexuality but allows people to read in to the sermon where they are. This inductive model of preaching gives hearers credit for making the connections with their own lives and the truth that they are facing or not facing. In a case like this it is not so important whether the minister shares his truth or even his struggle. What is important is allowing the gospel to be heard.

The sermon dances up to the edge of truth and stops short. Lucy Rose, in her homiletical study *Sharing the Word,* offers advice on how to deal with "truth" and Truth in a sermon. Advocating for a conversational method of preaching in which the preacher and the listener are discerning God's word together, Rose encourages preachers to write sermons out of their personal experience, but not to the exclusion of recognizing that it is not a universal experience: "Absolute truth is inaccessible; we preachers must be content with 'little truths' which are partial and personal, but which must be placed in conversation with those Truths that can enlarge and reconfigure it."[25]

Landis's exegesis of Luke 4:21–30 leads the hearer to believe that telling the truth — as Jesus did by reading the Isaiah scroll about his mission — is part of the Christian path. He builds on how telling one's truth can open doors to more intimacy, which can be dangerous territory. Those in Jesus' hometown heard him read their sacred text as if he were the One to fulfill the prophecy, and it angered them. It set their principles on edge by opening doors they did not necessarily want opened. Landis acknowledges that Jesus passed through them, and they were left with a gaping hole in their midst. By doing so, he honors how truth telling can be destructive initially as people face truth at varying levels within themselves. In addition, his sermon aims to encourage its hearers to try truth telling. His interpretation has to do with how Christians are to be telling their truth to one another as led by the Spirit.

However, it is interesting to note that while the sermon focuses on Luke 4:21–30, verses 16–30 are part of a larger section titled in the NRSV "The Rejection of Jesus at Nazareth." Since the theme of rejection is huge among gay and lesbian Christians who have tried to come out in the church and been rejected, had the sermon been

---

25. Lucy Atkinson Rose, *Sharing the Word: Preaching in the Roundtable Church* (Louisville: Westminster John Knox Press, 1997), 15.

preached by an out clergyperson, this theme would have resonated particularly with many in the LGBT community. In a way, Jesus coming to his hometown, speaking to his family, friends, and congregation about what his mission is, finds himself without a place to call home.

Jesus was not welcome in his hometown, but he had the courage to pass through the midst of them knowing that his strength and consolation came from God. This understanding is supported by biblical scholar Marcus Borg, who describes Jesus as a "Spirit person," in his book *Meeting Jesus Again for the First Time.* After an explanation of what it means to be a "Spirit person" Borg writes, "Jesus' experience of the Spirit is expressed with dramatic simplicity in the 'inaugural address' in Luke with which he begins his ministry: *'The Spirit of the Lord is upon me.'* At the center of Jesus' life was a profound and continuous relationship to the Spirit of God."[26]

Resurrection

Traditional theology has defined resurrection as the victory of life over death — decisively in the raising of Jesus from the dead. As a central theological tenet of the church, Jesus' resurrection was achieved by God's power over death and sin bringing opportunity for new life in Christ. For some Christians, belief in a bodily resurrection is tantamount to one's faith in Christ. Others agree God's sovereignty is displayed in the gospel's witness of Jesus' resurrection, but do not place significant emphasis on the form that it takes. While theologians continue to differ on bodily resurrection or symbolic resurrection, biblical writers made no distinction between soma (body) and the soul, like later theologians who were influenced by dualisms in Greek thought. When preaching resurrection, the focus is usually on the activity of God in Jesus' reappearance after his death, as told in each of the Gospels. The basic creed of Reformed churches is the Apostles' Creed,

---

26. Marcus Borg, *Meeting Jesus Again for the First Time* (San Francisco: Harper-Collins, 1995), 36.

which states a belief in the bodily resurrection of Jesus. The emphasis on belief has only limited our participation in the activity of resurrection in this life. In most liturgical churches (Roman Catholic, Eastern Orthodox, and Anglican) the Nicene Creed is more familiar. Its focus is not on the bodily resurrection, but on the resurrection of the dead. This way of thinking about God and our faith regulates the powerful activity of resurrection to afterlife — that when we die, we will be resurrected in some form, whether bodily or symbolically. Infrequently has resurrection been located within the individual Christian life in the here and now. Yet in liberation theology resurrection is both a metaphor for hope in Christ and a practice of one's faith here in this life. Exiled Guatemalan poet Julia Esquivel writes about resurrection of her people in her book *Threatened with Resurrection*. She parallels the suffering of Guatemalan peasants with the suffering of Christ and proclaims that they too will rise with life, that their blood has not been shed in vain. Hers is a theology of hope that despite death being the final word, resurrection is the greater accomplishment: "I die a thousand times and am reborn another thousand through that love from my People, which nourishes hope."[27]

~

The following sermon is included in a book about preaching and resurrection, *Risking the Terror: Resurrection in this Life.*[28] In it, professor of homiletics Dr. Christine M. Smith argues for a new reading of resurrection as an ongoing process in the human decisions we make and actions we can take that bring God's eternal power of life into the here and now rather than merely following a physical death, as it is traditionally understood in Christianity. In the context of LGBT oppression, Smith examines a new meaning of resurrection. Employing a typical resurrection text used at Easter time, in which the disciples

27. Julia Esquivel, *Threatened with Resurrection* (Elgin, IL: Brethren Press, 1982), 65.

28. Christine M. Smith, *Risking the Terror: Resurrection in This Life* (Cleveland: Pilgrim Press, 2001), 82.

are hiding and Jesus comes to them, Smith parallels this to lesbians and gay men who are hiding out of fear and the presence of Jesus in their midst.

Sermon:
"RESURRECTION — CALLED FORTH
FROM PLACES OF HIDING"
by Christine M. Smith

Text: John 20:19–29

Hear these challenging words from Jack Pantaleo reflecting on the death and resurrection of Jesus:

> In the life of Christ, we encounter this ultimate sacrifice. Jesus, as we all know, sacrificed his life. Nailed down to a cross and crucified, he gave up his very life, echoing his own words that one can have no greater love than to give up one's life for a friend. What an extraordinary sacrifice that was! Yet it was not the ultimate sacrifice, for if Jesus had stopped there, he would be remembered only as another nice teacher who spoke about love.
>
> Let's face it: death has been done before. Anyone can die. Jesus revolutionized creation because he had the nerve it took not to remain dead. Christ went beyond sacrificing his life. He sacrificed his death. He voluntarily let go of the comfort of death and fought to rise above the grave. The hardest thing we can do is not to die, but to live, and to live abundantly in joy.[29]

It is no coincidence that a gay man describes resurrection as a sacrifice of death — voluntarily letting go of the comfort of death. Pantaleo writes these words because he knows something very profound about closets, hiding places, locked doors, those places

---

29. Jack Pantaleo, "The Opened Tomb," *The Other Side* 28, no. 2 (March–April 1992).

that give needed security and protection, yet are ultimately places of stifling, suffocation, death. He also knows something deep and hopeful about fighting to rise above the grave, for he writes these words shortly after a time in his life when he was brutally raped by a stranger. He is struggling for his life. He is determined to sacrifice the dimensions of death that keep him from the promise and possibility of life.

What an extraordinary image of resurrection: the act of sacrificing death. Jesus had been spit on and mocked. He had been betrayed by loved ones and misunderstood by friends. He had been broken to the point of wondering if God had forsaken him and, finally, tortured, murdered. In the face of this, death might just be a blessed ending. But Jesus sacrifices the comfort of death to return for a time to those he loves. He appears to his disciples and friends, not just to reassure and console. He appears to them to call them forth from their places of hiding back into the world. He comes asking them to voluntarily let go of the comforts of denial, escape, closed doors, and to live, to live abundantly in joy.

"When it was evening on that day, the first day of the week, the doors of the house where the disciples had met were locked for fear. . . ."

Fear is a powerful and strange thing in our lives. It prompts us to seek protection in times of very real danger. It motivates us into needed changes and surprising adventures. It serves as a constant reminder that we are fragile, limited, and human. In contrast to these life-giving impulses of fear, we know fear can also immobilize us, cause us to "lock the doors" of our lives, and run away from life into places of isolated hiding.

Very few human emotions are as strong as fear. Very few experiences are as overwhelming and disorienting as those moments in life when we feel genuinely afraid. These early followers of Jesus are hiding for good reason. They are afraid. They have seen Jesus brutally murdered and were helpless to stop it. They know they could be next. It would be reasonable to expect Jesus to encourage them to get out of Jerusalem and hide anywhere they could. But no, he does not just come to call them forth. He comes to tell them to feed and tend all God's people, to preach the gospel to the whole creation, and to receive the power of the Holy Spirit.

His mandates are relentless, even after his death. The disciples cannot escape them. Even in the midst of being terrified and lost, even in the midst of their reasonable, justifiable fear, he calls them to abundant life. Jesus sacrifices the comfort of his own death, and he commissions them to do the same. He calls them to open the doors of their lives and to come forth from their places of hiding.

Jesus comes as absolute assurance that the power of God raised him right out of the grave and will be with them also. It is the greatest assurance and the greatest promise he can give them.

Why, after he appears as the resurrected one to some of the disciples in this place of hiding, are they still in that same place of hiding eight days later? Resurrection life, life that leaves the tomb empty and grave clothes undone, is not always such a glorious and joyful thing. Resurrection life, life that speaks our name and commissions us to speak its power to others, is rarely embraced by us with abandonment. Resurrection life, life that holds out wounded hands and pierced bodies and invites us to see and touch, is seldom what we would boldly choose.

The mystery and gift of resurrection are that, although it cannot be fully understood or possessed, it is utterly tangible. The disciples are not transformed by some intellectual notion of resurrection. Their lives are changed by the concrete reality of the presence of Jesus among them. I find it strange that so many interpretations of this particular resurrection story over the years have named it as a story about doubting Thomas because of his need for tangible signs of Jesus' resurrected presence. Thomas simply asks to experience what Jesus has so freely given to the others. Jesus knows that in the days and years ahead they will need the power of resurrection to face the forces that will threaten them with silence and death.

The more I think about courage that is required of us to face the claims and expectations of resurrection life, the more admiration I gain for Thomas. It is true he wanted and needed to see Jesus' hands and side. Who of us would not have needed this same reassurance? I can relate readily to this need.

What is amazing and somewhat shocking are Thomas's words: "Unless I see the mark of the nails in his hands, and put my finger in the mark of the nails and my hand in his side, I will not believe." Unlike the other disciples who simply see, Thomas longs to come close, to embrace, to touch. Thomas knows his own human limitations and boldly asks for what he needs. Maybe he knows that once he comes this close, he will never be the same.

I wonder what would change in our world if more of us were willing to put our fingers in the mark of the nails that crucify people daily and put our hands in broken and wounded sides? Resurrection life can be so palpable, so real, it promises to change us forever. Jesus does not condemn Thomas. He simply says, "Have you believed because you have seen me? Blessed are those who have not seen and yet have come to believe."

Is it not the same for us? Does it not take a human face, a particular voice, a concrete need to compel us to sacrifice the comforts of death, the graces of denial, apathy, isolation, and to move us closer toward abundant life?

Oscar Romero, archbishop of El Salvador, was moved toward resurrection by the lives and faces of his own people. Their brutal repression just kept finding him despite the locked doors of the church hierarchy and the hiding he tried so hard to do.

Dorothy Day, founder of the Catholic Worker movement, was moved toward resurrection by the homeless and hungry on the streets of New York City who were only asking for a simple meal, a place to rest, and some small portion of hospitality.

Daniel Berrigan, priest of peace, was moved toward resurrection by the images of an annihilated world and the destruction of all our children, both of which compelled him into civil disobedience against the production of nuclear weapons.

AIDS activists in ACT-UP are moved toward resurrection by the ravaged bodies of loved ones and the community's valuing of life. Both things drive them into the streets and churches to demonstrate against a system that appears so indifferent to human life.

Resurrection is not just something that happens to us after we leave this life as we know it. Resurrection is something that happens in profound ways in our everyday lives. It is not something that only comes at the end of Lent, at the end of struggle and death, but it can come and does come in the very midst of it

- for all of us to know more fully the graves we live in without even knowing.

- for us to believe in God's power that can radically renew and transform our collective lives.

- for the courage to come forth from places of hiding.

Analysis

Christine M. Smith speaks out of her lesbian experience. In her social analysis of heterosexism, Smith sees the problem is with the churches, not the presence of lesbians and gays: "I do not see homosexuality as the problem that needs to be addressed. In contrast, I see the church's condemnation of lesbians and gay men as the major pastoral and theological problem."[30] She writes about this in *Preaching Justice*, and includes the analogy of Lazarus's coming back to life and the untying of his grave clothes, which is the experience of many lesbian and gay people when they come out — the experience of a new life and resurrection.

A biblical text often theologized among lesbian and gay people is the raising of Lazarus (John 11:28–44). We know something

---

30. Smith, *Risking the Terror,* 90.

distinct about the tomblike quality of closeted existence, and we know something very concretely about the mandate given to those who loved Lazarus, "Unbind him, and let him go." The grave clothes of heterosexism and homophobia are legion, enough so that all of us could spend a lifetime untying them. And lesbian women and gay men know that untying the grave clothes of closeted living is absolutely impossible without a community of resistance and support. Preaching justice in solidarity with lesbian and gay people will challenge heterosexual people to develop the skills of untying grave clothes.[31]

Smith weaves the story of a man's recovery from rape with the Scripture from John's Gospel about the experience of meeting the resurrected Jesus behind closed doors. She uses social hermeneutics and analysis to inform this sermon; thus it is a social act. It seeks to name the pain and struggle of LGBT people and others in places of hiding. It offers a new rendering of "resurrection" as a Christian theme by reframing it as "giving up death." Smith bases this reframing on a writing done by a gay man struggling with being raped, who realizes that he has to "give up" the death of that experience in order to live again. It is a profound theological shift from thinking that Jesus' resurrection is the only resurrection to identifying how it is possible in our lives to experience resurrection — how coming back from dead places in our lives offers new life. It offers a radical way to think about Jesus' death and resurrection again. It offers solid theological ingredients for standing up against oppression and violence toward LGBT people in the Christian framework. This is an example of looking at Scripture from a new perspective that happens to be a lesbian one. In contrast to Stuart's queer theology, Smith's sermon is concrete as it locates one gay man's struggle from terror to resurrection. Rather than relying on baptism or communion as a means of salvation, as Stuart suggests,

---

31. Christine M. Smith, ed., *Preaching Justice: Ethnic and Cultural Perspectives* (Cleveland: United Church Press, 1998), 148–49.

Smith argues for our energy and action in the world to be toward God
for resurrection in this life.

Of course the sermon aims to transform those who hear and respond to it. But it also makes a social statement about the violence
toward gay people. It describes people who, in the past, have been
able to resist oppression and make room for resurrection life to enter
the community. Then she asks the hearer what it would take to move
us out of our hiding places, to put our hands into the world's wounded
side, and to touch the "other" as an act of grace. The sermon envisions
how living a resurrection life can be powerful, but it cautions, as well,
about the dangers of coming out of places of hiding. It invites — no,
pushes — the hearers to action in spite of that danger because that is
the call of God in Christ. At the same time, the sermon promises that
the God who calls us will not abandon us on the journey.

Resurrection, incarnation, and creation have come out with a new
song. Singing about the body, bodily contact, and embodied faith
from a same-sex experience is a new tune. Not everyone can sing
it yet. It will take time for churches to learn the tune. Prophetic sermons including these theological tunes will move the church forward.
Through claiming our Christian faith and practice, while speaking
honestly about our lives and love, we who have so long been hidden,
ignored, shunned, and marginalized, have swept the cobwebs from our
theological closets and come out. Standing, speaking, preaching, and
acting within Christian communities as a sexual minority is a difficult
journey for individuals and even more so for the church at large that
struggles with its own coming out process.

Lesbian, gay, bisexual, transgender, and queer theology is still in
the making. These theologies created by courageous women and men,
their voices, like raindrops hitting a pond, continue their rippling ef-
fects throughout Christian churches worldwide. Their sermons aid
the process of God coming out of a heterosexual-only paradigm. Embracing a broader understanding of sexuality in the church can be a
fresh wind that renews our faith. Liberal, liberationist, feminist, and
most recently postmodern theologies have been venues for this work.

There is still much on our to-do list of theological meaning making; we need to address sexual ethics, intolerance and torture of sexual minorities, our political voice, our wealth in relation to the world's LGBTQ culture, and the next generation of queers.

When lesbian women and gay men, bisexuals, transgender folk, and those who call themselves queer invest in the church, we are helping to redeem it from its idolatry of heterosexism and homophobia. By this, LGBT Christians witness to God and God's grace, which includes sexual orientation but also goes beyond it. Theological practice and preaching by LGBT clergy, allies, and welcoming churches will shift boundaries of theological understanding to places that are more spacious. In my vocabulary, the word "spacious" is another word for the theological concept of "salvation." Salvation means health, wholeness, and a spacious, safe place. The biblical meaning for salvation deals with the whole person and persons becoming whole. Concerned with the rifts in church and society he had witnessed in Nazi Germany, theologian Paul Tillich wrote about the meaning of salvation: "Healing means reuniting that which is estranged, giving a center to what is split, overcoming the split between God and ourselves, ourselves and our world, as well as the splits within ourselves."[32] Many in the Christian church (Roman, Orthodox, and Protestant) are estranged from people who identify as lesbian, gay, bisexual, and transgender. They may also be estranged from their bodies, from their sexual expression and intimate relationships. This separation keeps us from the embodiment of God in Christ. Queer theology extends a message of healing and salvation to Christians estranged from their bodies, from intimacy and sexual expression. On this matter, in a queer sort of way, it is the church that needs salvation more than the LGBT community.

---

32. Paul Tillich, *Systematic Theology*, vol. 1 (Chicago: University of Chicago Press, 1951), 166.

Chapter 5

Preaching Comes Out

Then Jesus said to Mary Magdalene and the other Mary, "Do not be afraid; go and tell my brothers to go to Galilee; there they will see me." (Matthew 28:10)

Go into all the world and proclaim the good news to the whole creation. (Mark 16:15)

. . . that repentance and forgiveness of sins is to be proclaimed in his name to all nations, beginning from Jerusalem.

(Luke 24:47)

Jesus said to her, "Mary!" She turned and said to him in Hebrew, "Rabboni!" (which means Teacher). Jesus said to her, "Do not hold on to me, because I have not yet ascended to the Father. But go to my brothers and say to them, 'I am ascending to my Father and your Father, to my God and your God.'"

(John 20:16–17)

Since the resurrection of Jesus Christ, the good news has been kept alive by the proclamation of women and men. A small band of Jesus' followers, named "the Way" in Acts 9:2, kept the movement alive by telling others, and so the gospel has spread "to the whole creation." Indeed, without proclamation from the women who witnessed the empty tomb — Mary Magdalene, the other Mary, and then the disciples — how would the good news have traveled this far?[1] What today we call homiletical theories and methods of proclamation are in their most organic form simply telling another what we know about God through the life of Jesus. Not so much what we believe, but what we *know* through experience and engagement with the Christ, the Holy One, the Divine.

As the church, we gather together to hear the Word of God made flesh again in spoken words that are both terribly inadequate for the task and supremely effective in their ability to communicate God's presence among us. Whether we as preachers preach the "right words" or "right theology" or use the "right methodology," our sermons, through an encounter of the Holy Spirit, become God's Word. Furthermore, we rarely get any clues how these words, ideas, and illustrations are received by the listeners. Yet, it is our faith in God that compels our preaching, as W. E. Sangster wrote: "Preaching is a constant agent of the divine power by which the greatest miracle God ever works is wrought and wrought again. God uses it to change lives."[2] I would add it is the greatest miracle since the resurrection of Jesus.

Truth through Personality

Preaching in the twentieth century to a great extent was shaped by the voice of a preacher at the end of the nineteenth century. The Reverend Phillips Brooks, the rector of Trinity Church in Boston, was considered the best preacher in his day. His lectures at Yale on preaching in 1877 and collections of his sermons formed a legacy that influenced most twentieth-century preaching and homiletics. While he offered many insightful thoughts about preaching, one rises above

---

1. To Paul, Lydia, Timothy, Phoebe, Justin Martyr, St. Nina of Georgia, Clement of Rome, Origen of Alexandria, Augustine of Hippo, Julian of Norwich, Martin Luther, Anna Howard Shaw, Karl Barth, Howard Thurman, Harry Emerson Fosdick, Martin Luther King Jr., James Forbes, Gene Robinson, Barbara Brown Taylor, and Billy Graham, to name a few.

2. W. E. Sangster, *The Craft of the Sermon* (Philadelphia: Westminster Press, 1950), 16.

the others and is often quoted. Brooks gave preaching a new focus, that of the preacher in relation to truth, when he stated,

> Preaching is the communication of truth by man to men. It has two essential elements, truth and personality. . . . Preaching is the bringing of truth through personality.[3]

It is this phrase, "truth through personality," that has shaped theories and methods of preaching ever since. Rather than focusing on Scripture or exegesis or even theology, Brooks shifts attention to that of the preacher; the human voice and the human being. Continuing this trajectory, he affirms "human experience as the theatre of God's continuing revelation."[4] Reading further in his lecture series, we find Brooks again considering what he means by truth and personality: "It is to be a message given to us for transmission, but yet a message which we cannot transmit until it has entered into our own experience, and we can give testimony of its spiritual power."[5] Giving testimony of the message as we have witnessed or experienced it is where the power of preaching lies. If preachers simply transmit the message without personal engagement or experience, then preaching runs the risk of becoming a lecture and the gospel becoming doctrine. In Brooks's theology and methodology of preaching, the person/preacher is not separable from the message/sermon. Not that the preacher is the message in any way, but that the messenger has a relationship to the message that gives it form and shape.

The famous quotation by Brooks deserves further elaboration as we create an LGBT homiletic. Brooks's understanding of preaching as "truth through personality" correlates with my theory that when a preacher who is openly lesbian or gay, or LGBT-supportive (queer), preaches in a predominantly straight congregation, then his or her very being communicates a truth before the preacher even opens his or her mouth. In communication theory it is widely understood that

---

3. Phillips Brooks, *On Preaching* (New York: Seabury, 1964), 5.
4. Ibid., 5.
5. Ibid., 14.

70 percent of all communication is nonverbal, that our body speaks a language all its own. The remaining 30 percent is voice, words, ideas, illustrations, stories, and so on. Perhaps I am especially aware of this because of my hearing loss in the human voice range. Since I was a young girl, I have relied on reading the body, the physique, the nonverbal communication of persons, and it has directed my attention to what is being said without words per se. It is not necessary to have this disability to intuit nonverbal communication. Most of us pay attention to this through sensing or intuition. It is what we pick up in human communication; we "know" without being "told." There is truth we carry in our bodies as sexual beings whether we are conscious of it or not. As lesbian and gay ministers and preachers, we tend to be more aware of this as a result of our coming out process. In our specific difference, God is in our lives, actively and profoundly, bringing fresh winds of healing to our knowledge of sexuality and relationships through the LGBT community.

By the same token, a preacher who is known by the listeners to be identified as a lesbian woman or gay man brings an added dimension to their preaching. The preacher has spoken through the mere presence of her/his being or personality. One could debate Brooks's meaning of personality and whether it includes the body in its physical and sexual realm, but in my reading from his lecture entitled "The Preacher in His Work," he does address the meaning fully. Brooks outlines in four points how a preacher is to do his or her best work, the third point being to "be profoundly honest." The final point is an admonition to be vital and alive, and to do everything to keep your vitality at its fullest: "Even the physical vitality does not dare to disregard . . . full red blood in the body; full honesty and truth in the mind; and fullness of a grateful love for the Savior in your heart."[6] As best I can ascertain, in Brooks's time, personality involved morality as well as the physical body. My definition of personality today encompasses not only those aspects but psychological and sexual well-being too.

---

6. Ibid., 107.

A Whole Body Preaching

With this reading of "truth through personality" in mind, a gay and lesbian homiletic includes the experience of one's body, including sexual expression — in this particular case, a sexual expression other than heterosexuality. For so long, we have assumed incorrectly that every preacher is heterosexual — end of discussion. In fact, until the emergence of LGBT voices within the Christian pulpit, most of us probably never thought to wonder about the preacher's sexual life. For, as we know, the topics of sex and Christianity are not exactly friends. Sexuality was not addressed head-on until the last few decades, if ever. The long-standing tradition of men only as ministers, whether celibate priests or married men, fostered an image of God as either nonsexual or heterosexual, which has lasted to this day. Similarly, when men were the primary theologians and preachers, an image of God as male was created. When women sought ordination and similar recognition for their preaching, they were met with resistance and even refusal to acknowledge their gifts and experience. Eventually, as woman preachers joined the ranks of male clergy, bringing with them inclusive and feminine language for God, it was a jolt to the mainline denominations and was controversial for years; however, it helped to dismantle the idolatry of a male God. Likewise, in most mainline denominations today, we are seeing the same thing happening as LGBT people are ordained and invited to serve churches.

In his or her preaching, every preacher does reveal something about the nature of God. As Brooks aptly pointed out, there is something in the personal identity of the preacher that is "God-like." This concept I call "whole body preaching," where the identity of the preacher communicates something to the listeners with or without our knowledge. Stated another way, the preacher communicates something of his or her truth, directly or indirectly, through preaching without referring to it in words. Our bodies preach! Our voices and our words are important, but we are not detached from our bodies. Bodies have needs — including sexual ones — that remind us of our humanity and God's glory within us.

In one case, through dialogue between an openly gay minister and his congregation about his sermons, he reported that the respondents said his presence as an openly gay ordained minister gave them license to hear and appreciate the Bible in ways that they had never imagined. One woman said, "A woman in the pulpit can say things that a man can't say, even if the same words are used. The same is true with a gay or lesbian minister."[7] There is a private and personal nature to sexuality and sexual orientation that when brought into the arena of preaching — the realm of God — could cause a level of discomfort for some, but others, as indicated by the above quotation, seem to embrace it as freeing.

Being an openly lesbian or gay preacher is a two-edged sword. On the one hand it can extend our learning about God to new dimensions, new images, and new possibilities. On the other, preaching as out lesbian or gay clergypersons can be a detriment to the message if that is all listeners can see or hear. There is the risk of being perceived as preaching about "it" — homosexuality — rather than the gospel. These possibilities remain in tension as tasks of a lesbian and gay homiletic unfold.

Other Whole Bodies — Women, Blacks, Latinos

Historically speaking, it has been men, and primarily straight, white, married men, who have inhabited the pulpits of the Christian church. For most of us, this reinforced the assumption of God's maleness. The same can be said for God's assumed race (white) and sexual identity (straight). The authority carried in this status has created a bind for preachers from African American traditions, Latino traditions, women, differently abled/specially gifted, and now lesbian and

7. J. Bennett Guess, "The Words We Hear: Listening to Sermons from a Lesbian, Gay, Bisexual and Transgendered Perspective," diss., Chicago Theological Seminary, 2001, 40.

gay clergy (and others who would identify themselves in this category). Most of our preaching voices are dismissed, challenged, and often ignored as if children of a lesser God. Every person who is not a white, straight, married male (and some who are) has struggled to find his or her preaching voice and gain attentive listeners. In my research and experience with LGBT people our differences are God-given, worthy of the same status the prevailing paradigm receives.

For instance, in Henry H. Mitchell's book *Preaching as Celebration and Experience,* he abandons Aristotle's idea of appealing to reason and instead appeals to emotions. From his African American roots, he is not so much interested in the truth of an idea as he is in reinforcement of that truth through celebration, which includes passion, emotion, and intuition. Mitchell's style of preaching aims for the heart rather than the head. In reviewing Mitchell's homiletic, Paul Scott Wilson writes, "The entire being of the preacher embodies the message to the *whole person* in the pew."[8] The reference to whole body engagement in preaching is shared by others whose experience confirms "truth through personality" as a viable preaching perspective.

To borrow another phrase from communication theory that replicates Brooks's quotation, "the medium is the message" is to reaffirm that the one who speaks becomes part of the message.[9] Applied to preaching, imagine an ordained African American woman preaching on the text, "Wives, be submissive to your husbands as you are to the Lord. For the husband is the head of the wife just as Christ is the head of the church . . . , Husbands, love your wives, just as Christ loved the church and gave himself up for her . . ." (Ephesians 5:22–23, 25), at a clergy gathering of African Americans composed mostly of men. Then imagine her doing the same at an African American women's retreat. It would be a different hearing for the same text and sermon because the preacher and the listeners have certain political dynamics

---

8. Paul Scott Wilson, *Preaching and Homiletical Theory* (St. Louis: Chalice, 2004), 106.

9. Herbert Marshall McLuhan, *Understanding Media: The Extension of Man* (New York: McGraw-Hill, 1964).

going on. One scenario might be that men hearing a woman preacher talk about how to treat their wives could be challenging. They might hear it, but more than likely they will dismiss it altogether, saying, "No woman is going to tell me how to treat my wife." On the other hand, there might be men who would be interested in what a woman thinks about this particular text. At the women's retreat, hearing from a woman preacher on this text that has often been used to reinforce men's domination over wives might create a different response when none of their husbands (or at least no men) are present. The Scripture and sermon carry a message to be sure, yet who delivers the Word to whom plays an important role in what is heard or proclaimed.

To increase our sense of this importance, take the same text and have a white middle-class male preach to an affluent, well-educated congregation in which he is the guest preacher and their senior female minister is on vacation. Besides being a guest preacher, the context throws in many factors including the dynamics of gender, class, and economic status to the hearing of his sermon. It also illustrates the importance of the preacher's awareness of the sociopolitical context and knowing who the listeners are for any given sermon. These elements need to be considered because often the medium is speaking louder than the message. Scripture and sermon give meaning, but so do the context and identity of the preacher.

Hispanic preachers and authors Justo Gonzalez and Catherine Gonzalez writing on liberation preaching glean from their experience what has happened in similar situations. When preachers from a minority position are invited into a context that holds more power than their identity does, the authors report that Scripture is appealed to more frequently. Knowing that they don't have the benefit of societal approval or credibility, preachers from minority positions tend to turn to Scripture for more authority. Interesting to note, though, where this will lead those of us in the church:

> Yet many white male preachers remain oblivious to such considerations, unless they are thrown into the situation of preaching

to a minority church. The rest of the time, to be white and male seems to them to have no particular effect on the words spoken and heard. Women and minority preachers are generally more biblical in the preaching because they do not have the benefit of status conferred upon them by society at large. White males who decide to preach on the radical demands of Scripture may soon find themselves in a similar situation.[10]

The authors do not include LGBT preachers in their analysis of the marginalized, thus rendering us invisible as is typical in most resources for preaching and the church. When the powerful seek to marginalize those seeking to be obedient to Scripture, something prevents them from hearing preachers from sexual minorities. Is it the fear that their words will become marginalized and they will lose what privilege they have established?

In twentieth-century American church history, a major event took place that continues to redefine church life, practice, and theology. A United Church of Christ seminary student, William Johnson, came out as a homosexual and was ordained; his openly gay voice as a preacher entered the homiletical world. Since then, many more out lesbian and gay ministers are preaching, yet Christians have failed to notice or hear us. Why is this? My research in this country has discovered few LGBT academic and professional homiletical voices from clergy. Are we still too afraid to come out?

Certainly, our preaching is challenged when our sexual identity dominates the way straight people hear our sermons. Said another way, what happens when a preacher, who is openly lesbian or gay, faces a congregation that holds a privileged position (namely heterosexual) in society? How does a predominantly heterosexual congregation hear sermons preached by clergy who are openly lesbian or gay? What are the dynamics of power involved? What homiletical steps can be taken to overcome this stereotype of preaching about "homosexuality"?

---

10. Justo L. Gonzalez and Catherine G. Gonzalez, *The Liberating Pulpit* (Nashville: Abingdon Press, 1994), 68.

What are the strengths that openly lesbian and gay preachers bring to the church, especially for the LGBT population within our mainline denominations? With these questions in mind, we move toward the homiletical garden, first stopping to remember where we have been, then to seek others on this path as we discover what weeds need to be pulled, what needs to be planted and watered, what needs to be trimmed and pruned, and what is already blooming that we have not noticed.

Questions Arise from Personal Experience

Openly lesbian or gay preachers have been in the pulpit only a short time. And while there are more welcoming churches now, not all of the churches who call gay/lesbian pastors have sufficiently dealt with their heterosexism and homophobia for the preaching of their pastors to be effective among them. When any change occurs in the life of a church — for instance, the calling of a minister who is openly lesbian or gay — the change can disrupt church life, especially if the denominational stance is against the ordination of homosexuals.

Churches respond differently, as I can attest from my experience in two denominations: Presbyterian Church (USA) and United Church of Christ. In one case, I was called to serve as associate minister (as an open lesbian) to a newly ONA (Open and Affirming) United Church of Christ church, and several members left after my arrival. Those who opposed and stayed made it clear they did not want the "lesbian" pastor to visit them. In another church, my ministry there was after the congregation had lived with their ONA commitment for ten years. In that congregation, there was no disruption or departure of members. While still in the closet, I served a congregation that was open and liberal even though their denomination would not ordain out lesbian or gay clergy. Had I come out in that context, it would have put the church in an awkward position and my ordination at risk. In yet another parish, where the denomination's policy was "no self-avowed practicing homosexuals," I vowed not to "serve in silence" anymore.

I came out to the elders who hired me. They welcomed me and my partner to live in the manse next door and stood beside us when one member challenged my ministry there on the basis of my sexual orientation. The final example comes from my time as a seminary administrator in an ordained position. Serving while in the closet and in a denomination that was in the heat of a battle over the ordination of lesbian and gay men was not an easy ministry. Eventually, I was outed by a student to the president of the seminary who had hired me three years earlier. He then canceled my contract rather than renew it.

Contributions from Other Research

At least three doctoral dissertations have addressed preaching and LGBT people. The importance of preaching about inclusion of lesbian and gay people was studied by Rev. Dr. Arlene Nehring in 1995. Her study included five UCC congregations that were going or had gone through the Open and Affirming process. Her hypothesis was, "that preaching matters in the ONA process, and by implication, that preaching plays an influential role in a congregation's work for social justice."[11] There is agreement that preaching is central to a congregation's knowledge of and engagement with issues of oppression. Preaching, in this case, shaped the congregation's response to the presence of LGBT people in the Christian church. Concurrently, had preaching or the preacher's approach sought to deny or dismiss the presence of lesbian, gay, bisexual, or transgendered people within the church, the response probably would have been to vote against the Open and Affirming welcoming statement. In her conclusion, Nehring states, "The practical-theological dialogue does not stop with an affirmative vote on an ONA statement.... Such dialogue commences

---

11. Arlene K. Nehring, "Hearts Open Slowly: Helpful Approaches to Preaching for UCC Pastors Whose Churches Seek to Become 'Open and Affirming'" (D.Min. diss., United Theological Seminary, Twin Cities, excerpts published in *Prism* [1995]: 75–93).

with the daily tasks of living out shared beliefs...by the congregations' ongoing efforts to achieve justice with — and on behalf of — lesbigay people."[12]

Over a decade later, my hypothesis reiterates that an affirmative ONA vote or statement in a congregation does not in any way ensure there is reasonable understanding of homophobia and its counterpart, heterosexism. As my research shows, we need to pay attention to the particularities of lesbian and gay clergy in their preaching roles in congregations that have approved an ONA statement. Even when a majority of members vote to become welcoming of LGBT people, having a clergyperson who is out can be altogether a different reality. Certainly this research is neither extensive nor conclusive, and it would help to have more input from preachers who are openly lesbian and gay and their congregations.

One such study by an openly gay UCC minister used the relationship with his congregation to study his sermons' effect on the listeners. Rev. J. Bennett Guess, in his dissertation, reports on interviews of his members which sought to understand their responses to his sermons' content, theology, and style. Guess offers twelve suggestions for preachers to follow for "Liberation Preaching" as a means of reaching LGBT listeners.[13] First, he writes, is to assume the broadest possible audience, meaning that whether you know it or not, there are LGBT people in the congregation. Liberation preaching means taking risks and being vulnerable in the pulpit. Liberation preaching knows the value of words — they can heal and harm, they can be cheap and concrete, and so care needs to be taken in sermons. The biblical basis for Guess's liberation preaching model comes from Acts 8:26–40, Philip's transforming encounter with the Ethiopian eunuch. Guess sees "this biblical image as a metaphor for preaching to marginalized persons, especially the homiletical issues inherent in preaching in solidarity with LGBT persons."[14] He also notes that effective preaching

---

12. Ibid., 93.
13. Guess, "The Words We Hear," 44.
14. Ibid., 9.

for LGBT listeners is not issue based but relationship oriented, which strengthens my whole body theory. The emerging lesbian and gay homiletic will include LGBT listeners and also the majority of church members who are straight.

A more recent dissertation studies the theological content of fifty sermons preached in various denominations that are welcoming of LGBT people. MCC pastor and author Mark Lee explains:

> My hope was to discern the outlines of a glbt-specific theology.
> I had hoped to find commonalities in the vision of God, Christ,
> salvation, and Christian hope. What I found however, was that
> even if those themes were present in the sermons they were
> not the primary issues that preachers were addressing. Preachers
> were preaching to where people itch. The core issues addressed
> were not theological questions per se, but rooted in the life
> experiences of the congregations.[15]

Measuring how frequently and at what depth a theological theme was expressed in a sermon, Lee's research identified five topics addressed most often in the sermons: (1) development of Christian community, (2) development of a healthy personal identity as a LGBT person and as a Christian, (3) justice — a Christian way of responding to oppression in the larger culture, (4) "nuts and bolts" of relationship, and (5) Christian living. This dissertation offers a fine detailed analysis of theological themes that are preached in congregations composed of primarily LGBT Christians.

A Whole Body Plus Spoken Words

As gay men and lesbians write more, publish more, preach more, teach more, and take public stands, a collective body of wisdom is emerging for gay, lesbian, and straight preachers. This wisdom applied to the

---

15. Mark Lee, "Hearing the Eunuch's Children: Preaching in Gay, Lesbian, Bisexual and Transgender Communities," D.Min project, Iliff School of Theology, 2006.

homiletical task gives way to the big picture. Our ultimate aim, the purpose of all preaching, is to bring God out of the closet of our spiritual lives. By this, we roll the stone away and let Jesus come to life in ways we never imagined. A sermon at the end of this chapter further elaborates on this theological idea of Jesus not being where we expect him to be. That God shows up in the lives of LGBT clergy through our sermons underscores this idea.

To create a lesbian and gay homiletic, I suggest there are four hall-marks, using the model of Martin Buber's relational theology: I–Thou. These will expand the concept of I-Thou for out LGBT preachers and our allies. American liberation theologian Robert McAfee Brown translates the concept of Buber's I-Thou relationship:

> Martin Buber is widely know for reflections on what he calls an "I-Thou" relationship between two human beings, in which each treats the other as a subject with whom there can be full reciprocity and sharing, in contrast to an "I-It" relationship, in which the other is reduced to an "object" who can be manip-ulated and used and is thus depersonalized from a "thou" to an "it." So much is well known. What is less well known, but equally important, is Buber's claim that any real "I-Thou" rela-tionship points to, and is grounded in, the Eternal Thou. Truly to enter into relationship with another human being is to enter into relationship with God.[16]

Entering into relationship with God through our relationships with others is at the heart of Hebrew Scripture and the New Testament. This is the central focus of an LGBT homiletic.

For purposes of this model, the "I" will represent the preacher, who in our context is out as a sexual minority (lesbian, gay, bisexual, transgendered, or queer) or out as an ally of sexual minorities but who is a member of the majority. Rather than rewriting this every

---

16. Robert McAfee Brown, *Spirituality and Liberation: Overcoming the Great Fallacy* (Philadelphia: Westminster Press, 1988), 105.

time when referring to the preacher, the "I" will be representative of those who are, by God's grace, an open witness to the Christ within the queer community.

The four hallmarks are:

1. I-Bible / Theology, the preacher in relation to the Bible and theology

2. I-Thou / You, the preacher in relation to the other, the Eternal Thou

3. I-Us / Justice, the preacher in relation to human communities in the larger world

4. I-Spirit / Intimacy, the preacher in relation to self, God, and intimacy

Together these are the stepping stones to a queer homiletic where sermons are created. For in our best efforts, whenever we preach, God comes out!

I-Bible / Theology

The first task, I-Bible / Theology, seeks to rethink biblically and theologically the images of God we preach as related to heterosexism and homophobia. The Bible as the Word of God is central to our preaching. This initial task invites preachers to think biblically and theologically about the process of coming out for LGBT people (chapter 2) while applying the tools we have acquired in exegesis and theology (chapter 3). Without repeating what these two chapters offer, one additional aspect of biblical and theological work needs highlighting. It involves a critique of liberation models of theology.

Our sermons will be immersed in biblical stories, images, and models of faith that empower and inspire listeners in developing their relational faith in God. An occasional use of a text of terror for educational purposes is possible, but a greater value is placed on passages where human encounters with God prevail. Employing a liberation model of reading the Bible needs to be balanced with relational accountability. Freedom for freedom's sake will ultimately meet its limitations. When Israel was freed from slavery in Egypt, there were freedom songs on the banks with Moses and Miriam (Exodus 15). But then, when unhappiness followed, where was water to drink and food to eat? For what purpose is this liberation from slavery if only to die in the wilderness, they asked. In the first of many replies to their cries, the Lord says to the Israelites, "If you will listen carefully to the voice of the Lord your God, and do what is right in his sight, and give heed to his commandments and keep all his statutes, I will not bring upon you any of the diseases that I brought upon the Egyptians; for I am the Lord who heals you" (Exodus 15:26). Liberation is coupled with obedience. Freedom is accompanied with responsibility. God invites Israel into relationship through the keeping of commandments and to "do what is right in his sight." Jesus brings this message to bear upon his teachings as well. When asked, "What must I do to enter the kingdom of heaven (or eternal life)," Jesus replies, "Love the Lord your God with all your heart, mind and soul, and love your neighbor as yourself." Liberation, being set free, is one side of the coin. Responsibility, what we do with that freedom, is the other side.

I-Thou/You

Second, a queer homiletic emphasizes the I-Thou/You relationship between the preacher and the other. This includes the preacher's position of power, recognizing God in ourselves, and our exercise of power. Specifically, this means to acknowledge the different levels of power as related to our sexual orientation in the community. For clergy who are out lesbians or gay men serving congregations, we have moved from the margins of church life to its center, as we become preachers in congregations that are primarily heterosexual. For closeted LGBT clergy, this means they retain their power yet sacrifice their personal life and integrity. For clergy who are straight allies, their position of power as a heterosexual who speaks on behalf of LGBT people might create a reverse position. They may move from the center of power to the margins where there is less power. As pastor and congregation build a relationship, it will be important to talk about heterosexual privilege. The purpose is to develop an understanding about power differences that might alleviate problems later. For our straight allies who openly stand with the LGBT people, bless same-gender relationships, or support the ordination of clergy who are openly lesbian and gay, this homiletic risks their power. Their position of power as a straight person could shift to the margin as they preach the gospel that welcomes the queer community.

To break out of the stagnant "it" description of homosexuals as an issue, preachers need to develop a community of hearers in the congregation committed to exploring their own homophobia/heterosexism. There are, of course, several ways to accomplish this, but all involve being in relationship with one another and thereby, God. They all involve being in a community of faith that seeks to know Christ in one another, and to follow the command to love God with all of our being and to love our neighbor as we love ourselves.

One possible exercise toward building relationships might be a church book group — inviting both straight and LGBT members to read together a book that relates to the personal lives of LGBT people. For instance, Leanne Tigert's book *Coming Out through Fire: Surviving the Trauma of Homophobia* or Chris Glaser's *Coming Out as Sacrament* are both good possibilities. In order to learn and grow, we need to become credible partners in genuine dialogue, and a book group offers one path. Composed of gay, lesbian, bisexual, transgendered, and straight members, the difficult process of learning to listen starts with our hearts. It's hard not to interrupt or speak over another person's story, especially when it makes us uncomfortable. However, very specific ground rules are important so that all members feel heard and have a chance to talk. Such rules might include (1) only one person talks at a time, sharing from their experience or belief, and when he or she finishes, a moment of silent reflection is given rather than an immediate response; or (2) that others who contribute shall not talk over another person's statement. Using a talking stick or some other device helps pace group conversation and allows it to move forward rather than becoming a debate between members. Also, it helps to have one person facilitate by watching time and allowing everyone to have a chance to say something. In consciousness-raising groups that are learning from a minority group, it is important to give more time to those who often have less voice or attention; in our context, this means letting the LGBT members talk first. In time, gay and lesbian members may want to tell their coming out experience. With all of its tears and joy, it can be the single most important contribution to increase understanding between LGBT and straight members. In my experience, such sharing allowed straight members to ask questions about homosexuality that they had never had the courage to ask, much less talk about at church. In turn, straight allies can be strengthened in their understanding and courage to speak up for gay and lesbian persons. As we know, in any liberation movement, the work includes more than just the oppressed. We need straight allies.

The recovery work done through such a book study can inform a lesbian and gay homiletical model. In a book of advice for preachers, homiletician Mittes McDonald de Champlain offers this: "Authenticity is the key term and the ultimate goal for communicating the gospel in our time." She goes on to define what she means by authentic: "being open, honest, relevant, and real," rather than "being dynamic, powerful, forceful, and eloquent."[17] Any reader of homiletics will note that the latter grouping of adjectives describes attributes popular in preaching years ago. When preaching held an authoritative place in the community in the early and mid-twentieth century, being dynamic, powerful, forceful, and eloquent was important. According to Champlain, the act of preaching today needs to offer a greater openness, honesty, and relevance in our sermons and our presence. This concerns the character of the preacher and the sermon. "To ring true

---

17. Mittes McDonald de Champlain, "What to Do While Preaching," in *Best Advice for Preaching*, ed. John S. McClure (Minneapolis: Fortress Press, 1998), 100.

while preaching, then, preachers will want their manner and mannerisms to be true to themselves and true to life."[18] This is certainly an issue for lesbian and gay clergy who want to be out and true to ourselves, but find that when we do, people's reactions interfere in our ministries and "it" — our sexuality — becomes the issue rather than ministry. For these reasons, a lesbian and gay homiletic must be as authentic and real as possible, realizing there is always the risk of being misunderstood.

For out lesbian and gay clergy serving predominantly heterosexual churches it will be an important strategy to have an ongoing group of members who are willing to listen, get to know gay and lesbian people, share experiences, and really get involved in public ways with one another. By doing this, both homosexual and heterosexual people realize there are similarities and differences in our common struggle to be human. Our commonalities bind us together more than separating us by our different sexual orientation. This may not seem like a preaching strategy, but it is. It is about engaging in honest talk, being open to God's Spirit, and listening with ears of God. Homosexuals and heterosexuals need to see this bonding activity happening in the community, for when a gay or lesbian clergyperson is called as the preacher, there will be support that goes further than just words, that is deeper and more relationally grounded. It is also about continuing to overcome internalized homophobia within all of us and to develop healing relationships that can lead to transformation within the church and society.

Straight clergy allies are in a better position to develop relationships with members not entirely supportive of people from the LGBT community. Building relationships with members as a vocal straight ally can open places of grace and understanding between people where an out gay clergy's voice would not be heard or welcomed. Historically, preaching against oppression has called upon those in positions

---

18. Ibid., 101.

of power and influence to take a stand with the oppressed and be willing to risk their position for the liberation of others.

History offers us a lesson in preaching: a white preacher, Rev. Colbert S. Cartwright, of Little Rock, Arkansas, preached against segregation in his white congregation in 1957. It was a bold move for a white person in the South to come out in support of desegregating the public schools at that time. He told the story of watching the first courageous young black girl walking down the street toward Central High School and what an impact that made on his life. It moved him so that he went to Elizabeth Eckford's home and asked her what gave her the courage to walk through the crowds of whites yelling for her to go away and worse. She replied, quoting Psalm 27 (KJV), "The Lord is my light and my salvation; whom shall I fear? The Lord is the strength of my life; of whom shall I be afraid?" Cartwright asked her a few more questions about her desire to go to Central High School. He learned that she wanted to go there to take classes her school did not offer, like debate, as she wanted to become a lawyer. To Elizabeth Eckford, and in his sermon to his white congregation, he said, "This week I've been ashamed to be a white person." "Why?" Eckford asked. "Because," I said, "it is we white people who have caused all your troubles. I'm ashamed."[19] It was presumably pivotal in the lives of his listeners to hear their minister speak on behalf of black people; as a white preacher, Cartwright was in a position of influence to spread the gospel net wider by sharing the faith of Eckford with his congregation.

Like many straight preachers of today, Cartwright was preaching for inclusion (African Americans in the once white schools) while his congregation was against it. He used his position of power and privilege to speak on behalf of those without a voice. Cartwright took a first-person-narrative approach that gave testimony from his heart about how he was changed. He brought truth through his personality

---

19. Joseph Jeter, *Crisis Preaching: Personal and Public* (Nashville: Abingdon Press, 1998), 145.

as a white male who witnessed the power of faith in this young black female.

Are we so courageous in our preaching today? A sermon offered at the end of this chapter by a United Methodist clergywoman who is straight gives a similar witness through a narrative as well as inductive approach to preaching. Her sermon invites listeners to imagine church life from a gay or lesbian member's perspective.

The I–Thou/You task of a queer homiletic examines the power dynamics that have occurred for lesbian and gay clergy who have moved from the margins into the pulpits of mainline denominations as ministers of congregations. Typically, when those who have long been on the margin or "in the closet" move to a center position, there is the risk of forgetting what it is like on the margin. The experience of oppression and marginality of gay men and lesbians will reshape theological categories, ethical understandings, biblical interpretation, and the practice of Christian ministry. In order for a lesbian and gay homiletic to be faithful to itself, it must remember what it is like to be on the margin, and keep a perspective on power that mirrors the experiences of LGBT people.

I-Us/Justice

In the third task, I-Us/Justice, a lesbian and gay homiletic chooses to come out on behalf of all people on the margins, exercising solidarity as Esther did with her people (chapter 3). A lesbian and gay homiletic seeks to address the oppression, violence, and inequality created by heterosexism. Stemming from enculturation, this lesbian and gay homiletic seeks to address the interrelated web of oppressions that afflict those with differences related to class, race, gender, ability, economic status, religion, and nationality. In this task, the preacher's awareness is directed to those on the margins in and beyond the church building. Having known pain in our lives, and having found a community of hope, we seek to be prophetic witnesses for others.

Preaching of this kind includes a social hermeneutic in the process of sermon writing — bringing the biblical word to bear on social situations like war, racism, sexism, poverty, ecological destruction, and violence. Preaching of this nature aims to interpret the present world through social analysis and then offer a new vision of what could be, of what and how God is calling us to live together. A social analysis or critique of our world or the church is a homiletical method, as preacher Christine Smith describes it:

> Preaching is an act of public theological naming. It is an act of disclosing and articulating the truths about our present human existence. It is an act of bringing a new reality into being, an act of creation. It is also an act of redeeming and transforming reality, an act of shattering illusions and cracking open limited perspectives. It is nothing less than the interpretation of our present world and an invitation to build a profoundly different new world.[20]

This homiletic method is direct and clear in its purpose. It seeks to lift up the brokenhearted, the marginalized, and the dispossessed, as well as LGBT people, who are in our midst and asks serious theological questions about our participation in their condition. This method addresses human suffering in all its manifestations and names the evil systems that perpetuate such suffering. Then it offers constructive ways to confront this oppression through honest confession, involvement, and resistance throughout the world.

As a balance to this approach, which leans on human activity as the primary source of hope in the world, Presbyterian professor Charles L. Campbell cautions that preaching on social issues can suggest that people of goodwill can solve these same problems. This can leave listeners feeling overwhelmed and guilty for what they are not doing

---

20. Christine M. Smith, *Preaching as Weeping, Confession, and Resistance: Radical Responses to Radical Evil* (Louisville: Westminster John Knox Press, 1992), 2.

or for what they do despite seeing no change. Similar to 2 Corinthians 4:7, "But we have this treasure in clay jars, so that it may be made clear that this extraordinary power belongs to God and does not come from us," Campbell asserts, "human weakness before the powers always reminds us that we rely on the power of God, not our own strength, in resistance."[21] Still Campbell advocates for "active resistance" to participating in systems of evil and places of privilege. Preaching in this country to congregations that are not oppressed, Campbell turns the coin and calls for redemption from captivity of mainline complacency.[22]

Social analysis preaching shares the rubric of liberation preaching. Justo L. Gonzalez and Catherine G. Gonzalez coined the phrase in 1980 in their book *Liberation Preaching: The Pulpit and the Oppressed*. One suggestion they offer for those who want to preach from a liberation perspective but who may not be in a setting that reflects the particular issue is to use imagination — to imagine a different setting. For instance, if a lesbian clergywoman wanted to preach to her ONA congregation on World AIDS Day about the injustices toward LGBT people worldwide using Psalm 23 as her text, she might try to imagine what it is like to be gay in South Africa versus what is it like to be gay in Holland. In Holland, there is more acceptance and freedom for sexual minorities than in South Africa. The preacher, in this method, seeks to apply the text in various settings to have it heard differently in other cultures, since in her own country homosexuality has crossed a cultural boundary. If she were to use her life in America as part of the sermon, it would not bring the real urgency of AIDS and injustice toward LGBT people worldwide into sharp focus. The imagery in Psalm 23 is resplendent with possibilities for imagination: green pastures, still waters, a valley of the shadow of death, an overflowing cup, and dwelling in the house of the Lord.

---

21. Charles L. Campbell, *The Word before the Powers: An Ethic of Preaching* (Louisville and London: Westminster John Knox Press, 2002), 91.

22. Ibid., 90.

It is worth stating again: the LGBT homiletic has an imperative to consider those on the margin besides LGBT people. Paul Scott Wilson in his critique of homiletical theories would place in the radical postmodern genre any homiletic that is primarily concerned with the marginalized.[23] Three of the seven key attributes of the radical postmodern school are those that strive for horizontal ideas of authority, focus on relationship over autonomy, and multiple meaning and interpretations of texts. These three can be seen clearly in *Sharing the Word: Preaching in the Roundtable Church*. Rose successfully argues the need for marginal voices to enter the homiletical conversation. She analyzes three dominant homiletical methods in use: deductive, inductive, and transformational, pointing out that each leaves questions unexplored. Her basic conviction is that preachers and congregations are equal partners (horizontal authority) on a journey to understand and live out their faith commitments together. Rose believed the task of preaching was for both the preachers and the congregations; they stand together (relationship over autonomy) to discover the meaning or mystery of a text. The use of "marginal voices" caught my attention in Rose's work. This arrangement of "equal partners" aims to keep power balanced between a preacher and the congregation. Rose hoped a conversational homiletic would foster a new power arrangement in preaching.[24]

In the lesbian and gay world, power is different because the male/female gender dynamic is not the same as in the heterosexual world. LGBT people also realize the need to cooperate within our community, to develop partnerships, and to create new arrangements of power since the old ones are not useful in our lives. We have discovered in our partnerships that intimacy is about mutual sharing of power in companionship, not about power over another, for that is the way God's love comes to us, in the humanity of Jesus who

---

23. Paul Scott Wilson, *Preaching and Homiletical Theory* (St. Louis: Chalice Press, 2004), 139.

24. Lucy Atkinson Rose, *Sharing the Word: Preaching in the Roundtable Church* (Louisville: Westminster John Knox Press, 1997).

journeys with us. Rose's homiletical theory of "a communal, heuristic and non-hierarchical understanding of preaching" does resonate with the LGBT homiletic in that it desires shared power and authority in community.[25]

I-Spirit/Intimacy

Finally, the fourth task, I-Spirit/Intimacy, revolves around self and Spirit, one's relationship with God, one's intimate relationship to self and another. Due to this, I want to share something of a personal nature to illustrate spirit and intimacy at work in preaching.

When I preached, I experienced this ecstatic feeling of sexual and spiritual energy. Was anyone else experiencing this, or was I just weird? I wanted to know. Who could I risk asking? I couldn't think of anyone who would both understand the tasks of preaching and the sexual energy I felt when I preached. Instead, I read books in search of another's similar disclosure. Just in time, Carter Heyward's book *Touching Our Strength: The Erotic as Power and the Love of God* was published.[26] Not that it directly answered the question in regards to preaching, but her work did confirm my sense that my love for God and my ability to express love in a physical/sexual way are connected. I was experiencing the erotic as sacred in the context of worship, but also in front of all these people! Perhaps that is why the ancient Hebrews called the inner sanctum of the temple "the Holy of Holies." It was where the ark of the covenant was kept, where Isaiah's vision took place — "the counterpart of God's heavenly throne room, the place where God's majestic presence was most powerfully felt. The 'spiritual voltage' there was so high that it was entered only once a year, on the Day of Atonement, and then by only one person, the high priest."[27] In

---

25. Ibid., 1.

26. Carter Heyward, *Touching Our Strength: The Erotic as Power and the Love of God* (San Francisco: Harper & Row, 1989).

27. Ellen F. Davis, *Proverbs, Ecclesiastes and the Song of Songs* (Louisville: Westminster John Knox Press, 2000), 240.

no way do I want to indicate that my experience is universal or necessary for understanding the link between sexual intimacy and God. Awareness of this connection comes in different ways.

The gift of conversation about sexual expression and God by LGBT people is unique to a lesbian and gay homiletic. Writing in her book *The Queer God*, Althaus-Reid describes this task too: "we need to begin a reflection intimately linked to a God-talk on loving and pleasurable relationships. This is one of the most important challenges that Queer theologies bring to theology in the twenty-first century: the challenge of a theology where sexuality and loving relationships are not only important theological issues but experiences which unshape Totalitarian Theology (T-Theology or I-It) while re-shaping the theologians."[28] Some LGBT theologians describe how sexual practice and spiritual practice are linked together — an important reflection for preachers.

One example of this is from a commentary on Song of Songs, where the sexual and the religious understandings of this book are mutually informative. In the author's view, Song of Songs is a celebration of faithful human love, not just sexuality, as some commentators have written. Davis writes:

> For a holistic understanding of our own humanity suggests that our religious capacity is linked with an awareness of our own sexuality. Fundamental to both is a desire to transcend the confines of the self for the sake of intimacy with the other. Sexual love provides many people with their first experience of ecstasy, which literally means "standing outside of oneself." Therefore the experience of healthy sexual desire can help us imagine what it might mean to love God truly — a less 'natural' feeling for many of us, especially in our secular society.[29]

---

28. Marcella Althaus-Reid, *The Queer God* (London and New York: Routledge, 2003), 8.
29. Davis, *Proverbs, Ecclesiastes*, 233.

Keeping attentive to the I-Spirit/Intimacy relationship is central for preachers in this homiletic. The development of an awareness of self and sexuality in relation to God deepens the ability to reflect this in body language as well as words in a sermon. Preaching about sexuality is not necessarily the goal; rather it is the ability to communicate through one's body and voice and words the acceptance of sexuality as a gift from God to be used as a movement toward God. Finding ways to illustrate and not exploit sex will be the challenge. In Guess's dissertation he reminds us that LGBT people are not looking for more information about sex. Instead, they want images of genuine love and faithfulness in relationships, including with God as the Lover.

Singing Sex and Gender

In addition to preaching, with awareness of sexuality, we sing sermons when we sing hymns. The theology of our hymnody needs to support the coming out theology in our sermons. Resources and new hymns are available. Imagine if the church sang hymns with LGBT–inclusive images of God, hymns that mentioned gay and straight together, and heard sermons by out lesbian and gay clergy. How might that shape the straight world we live in and provide an alternative reality for lesbian, gay, bisexual, and transgender people within the Christian tradition? Some have already asked these questions and are on the way to providing an answer, especially in the Metropolitan Community Churches, a predominantly LGBT denomination.

Toward this reality, at least two books published in recent years introduce hymns, prayers, liturgies, and other worship resources by, for, and in celebration of LGBT Christians. The Welcoming Church movement published *Shaping Sanctuary,* a collection of worship resources from a variety of submissions from denominations that participate in proclamation the gospel of love and grace that is not exclusively available to heterosexual people. The Welcoming Church movement is a transdenominational effort to articulate an LGBT theopolitical presence within mainline denominations. From the introduction:

Listening to LGBT lives . . . welcoming churches witness the face of Jesus Christ in the volunteer efforts of a Bisexual Sunday School teacher, the faithful service of a Transgender clergy-woman, the loving raising of a child by Lesbian parents, or the attentive care for the church building grounds by a Gay couple of twenty-two years. Welcoming churches have listened and discerned God in the lives of their LGBT neighbors. They have taken these lives seriously as statements of faith.[30]

This voice points us in the direction of an I-Thou relationship, rather than an I-It issue or problem. Research from a case study within the United Church of Christ supports this path over policies and even the "Opening and Affirming" processes. It is the relationship with one another that allows us to see the face of God.[31]

Many new hymns included in this volume refer to sexual orientation or relationship inclusion. An example is "For the Goodness of Our Bodies,"[32] which includes images that honor gay relationships. Written in 1997 by Ruth Duck, the hymn is set to the tune *El Camino*. Here are two of the verses:

> For the goodness of our bodies made for caring,
> For the longing of two hearts learning to love,
> For the joy that lovers find in one another,
> For these good gifts, we would thank you, loving God.
> For these good gifts, we would thank you, loving God.
>
> For the vows a man and woman honor daily,
> For the pledge two women keep with all their hearts,
> For the commitments two men keep with one another,

---

30. Kelly Turney, ed., *Shaping Sanctuary: Proclaiming God's Grace in an Inclusive Church* (Chicago: Reconciling Church Program, 2000), xii.

31. Della Fahnenstock, "Relationships, Not Policies Make Welcoming Churches: A Case Study in the United Church of Christ," 2000. See online *http://clgs.org/5/pdf/fahnenstock_relationships.pdf*.

32. Turney, *Shaping Sanctuary*, 271.

For these good gifts, we would thank you, loving God.
For these good gifts, we would thank you, loving God.

The second book, *Courage to Love,* is an anthology of worship ma-
terials from lesbian, gay, bisexual, and transgender men and women
around the world. The liturgical resources include same-sex blessings
and marriage ceremonies, baptismal and Eucharistic rites, poems and
prayers based on Scripture, and personal pieces that give witness to
faithful LGBT Christians from every land around the globe. Writing
about sexuality and God, one contributor from Hong Kong notes, "sexuality is crucial to God's design that creatures do not dwell in isolation
and loneliness but in communion and community. Through the incarnation, God not only participates in human sexual experiences, but
God is intrinsically sexual."[33] Thanks to Internet connections, LGBT
Christians throughout the world find each other and have become a
movement that is shaping a more inclusive and sexually aware church.

Another example of different images for God is reflected in a relatively new hymn. "Bring Many Names," composed and written in 1989
by Brian Wren, speaks of "aspects of the divine revealed in our maleness, femaleness, youth, and age, moving, growing matrix of God."[34]
Two of the verses shown here describe God in terms of gender with attributes normally associated with the opposite gender. For instance, we
usually associate the adjective "strong" with men and the adjectives
"warm, hugging" with women. Wren's juxtaposition of these adjectives challenges what we are used to thinking about gender. Then he
pushes further, applying the anthropological description of humanity
to God. These words create new images of God in our minds, and we
begin to see or experience God in unexpected places. Perhaps we see
God as nongendered, but a "genius at play" or "hugging every child."
These two verses relate to gender differences:

---

33. Geoffrey Duncan, ed., *Courage to Love* (Cleveland: Pilgrim Press, 2002), 184.
34. Brian Wren, "Bring Many Names," Hymnal Committee, *The New Century
Hymnal* (Cleveland: Pilgrim Press, 1995), 11.

Strong mother God, working night and day,
planning all the wonders of creation,
setting each equation,
genius at play:
Hail and Hosanna,
strong mother God!

Warm father God, hugging every child,
feeling all the strains of human living,
caring and forgiving
till we're reconciled:
Hail and Hosanna,
warm father God![35]

Playing with Wren's hymn, I have created another verse that includes the lives of lesbian and gay people and biblical references. How might these associations of gay experience in a hymn about God welcome those who recognize this as their lives? The same can be said for preaching; when lesbian and gay people preach, their experience comes through their lives and words. It may be challenging at first to hear God referred to as "queer," but the term can mean odd or different. It is not just a sexual term.

Fabulously Queer God, opening closet doors,
welcoming all the hidden ones with light,
sweeping for the lost coin,
rejoicing when found:
Hail and Hosanna,
rainbow color God.

◈

Two sermons by female clergy leaders now follow, one openly lesbian and the other openly straight. The contexts for their preaching are rad-

---

35. Ibid.

ically different. One is the pastor of a multiracial, open, and affirming inner-city church in San Francisco with a large population of sexual minorities. Bishop Yvette Flunder started this church, City of Refuge, and combines her Pentecostal background with UCC theology in her practice of ministry. She is openly lesbian and African American. The Reverend Susan Sumwalt-Patterson is senior minister of a United Methodist church in a predominantly white suburban church. She is married, white, and heterosexual. This church has a history of male pastors as senior ministers. Her denomination continues to debate the ecclesiastical gifts of LGBT people. She preached this sermon in her congregation and for a course at Iliff School of Theology. The first sermon, by Bishop Flunder, was given at the City of Refuge UCC and is also available online.

Sermon:
"SOMEONE HAS STOLEN JESUS"
Easter 2006
by Bishop Yvette Flunder

Text: John 20:10–15

"You see he died day before yesterday. . . . "

"We placed him in a snug comfortable tomb, secure from the elements and external influences. We put him where we could find him. All of his miracles are behind him.

"He's dead . . . and death is the end. All he could do he has done already. I loved him. I served him. I am here to maintain him. I did not come here for an event. I came to be alone one last time with my Jesus."

This woman was in deep grief and loss. Her future hopes were dashed. Her senses callused. She was worn out from the events of the last two days. And now Jesus was not where he was supposed to be. Jesus was not only dead but also missing. She knew they hated him. What might they be doing to the body of the one she loved so much? She came looking for her Jesus, and she was willing to go get him, pick him up, and carry him back to his tomb.

You see, a form of Jesus, a shell of Jesus is better than no Jesus at all.

At least she could look at the shape of his lips that spoke softly to her, the curve of his hands that touched and healed her and remember. . . .

She went to find the remains of her Lord to care for him as he had cared for her.

She knew it was over when he had been pulled from the garden and taken from judge to judge, handled by hateful hands and discarded as just another expendable religious fanatic.

And she loved him, but she did not really know who he was . . . or where he was. And on this morning of all mornings she needed him to be where he was supposed to be. It is great grief to those who know Jesus when the Jesus they know is taken away, or is transformed from the Jesus they were accustomed to. This is seldom thought of as a time to rejoice. Where was he? Who took him, and how could she get him back?

Could it be that her need to find Jesus where she left him hindered her from seeing where he was?

Can our need to keep Jesus where we need him blind us to where Jesus is moving today?

Can our need to confine Jesus keep us from participating in the real power of his resurrection? Do we waste our time by looking in a graveyard for a living, dancing, glorified Jesus?

Now let's not think little of Mary. She represents many who are loyal, vigilant, and faithful to attending a graveyard where Jesus used to be and asking, "Where have they taken him?"

"Where did you take him?" she asked.

Someone said, "We've got him. He's over here!"

"He now dwells behind stained glass and in the vaulted ceilings of mighty gothic cathedrals. He flies in buttresses. He resides in shrines and holy places . . . in relics and shrouds. He whispers a lot."

"No, we've got him!"

"Jesus is walking among things political and national. Jesus is the man. Proposition J. He is a plank on our platform. We put him back on the Supreme Court! He is on the banner that goes before us in war. . . . He supports preemptive strikes! He is here with us on the right. We sealed him up in our positions, our rallies, and our mass mailings. We've got him . . . we've dressed him up in prejudice. Made him hate the poor, the immigrant, and Mickey Mouse. He speaks very little . . . we talk for him."

And I hear a voice from the left. . . . "We really do have Jesus, but we've stripped him of most of his power, his glory, and his mystery. We made Jesus another great teacher, you know, like Gandhi, or Martin, or Nelson. We made Jesus more manageable. . . . We've got him under control."

It did not dawn on Mary that nobody took Jesus. She did not realize Jesus got up and got out of there himself. The living Christ does not dwell long where death is the lifestyle.

She didn't know that Jesus had come forth to usher in a new and living way.

Mary couldn't conceive that Jesus could be doing such a radical new thing. She loved him but she couldn't imagine the full scope of his power and influence.

She did not know that he could steal victory from his own death.

She did not know that she need not pity the Lord of Lords.

Mary couldn't imagine that death had been turned into life . . . and once death had tasted life again, no grave could hold it.

There are those of us who would prefer a dead Christ in his place to a living one outside of our control.

There are those who can only recognize Christ in certain forms and under certain circumstances.

Imagine the struggle for some quiet Protestant church folks watching some African American folks dancing in the spirit well into the night. I'm sure someone felt to ask the question, "How dare these people try to claim my Jesus?"

Imagine a group of patriarchal religious folks watching a group of men, women, and children who are not gender- or orientation-limited rejoicing in the Lord in perfect freedom. I'm sure someone would say, "What have they done with our Jesus?"

Can we hold him in our religions?

Can we keep Jesus in the church?

Can we even confine him to Christianity?

Into what sect, denomination, or order has Jesus crowded all the riches of heaven? Into which race, ethnicity, country, culture, gender, or orientation has Jesus poured out all of himself exclusively?

To whom has he given all the truth so that we may cease to seek him daily?

He's up now, out of the confines of the tomb. . . .

He's out now, and he will not be held exclusively, by anyone.

Just about the time we feel we have Jesus down to a science we see the wonder of his ability to show up in people and in places we never would have guessed possible. He is not back at the church where you left him. He is here with you.

Go get your Jesus back!

Go get your purpose back!

Marginalized people often feel alienated from God because they/we are alienated from religion. . . . "We can't do this or that because too many people are against us." But the battle is already won. . . . That is why the folk who oppose inclusion are so mad and desperate. They know it too.

Go get your parents back!

Go get your ministry back!

Go get your children back! No laws are going to stop us from caring for children.

No laws are going to stop Jesus from loving us or keep us from loving each other.

> IF WE SEEK TO CONFINE HIM
> BEHIND ANY WALLS . . . ANY STONE

HE WILL BREAK OUT EVERY TIME.
HE IS THE LIVING WAY.
HE IS THE LIVING TRUTH.
HE IS A FRESH-FLOWING RIVER.
HE IS RESURRECTION POWER.
HE IS LIGHT AND HE IS LIFE.
AMEN.

Analysis

Bishop Flunder tells the resurrection story from John's Gospel and continues into the sermon affirming that for which John's Gospel is known: the belief that Jesus is the Way, the Truth, the Light, and the Power. She uses strong biblical images and reinforces them with her closing, staying close to Scripture throughout the sermon. Flunder points to the liberating Jesus whom we cannot pin down no matter how hard we try and no matter if we are left or right, gay or straight. Her theology of liberation is tempered with responsibility in such statements as: "Go get your Jesus back! Go get your purpose back! Go get your parents back! Go get your ministry back!" Flunder, in analyzing her own theology for preaching, writes, "Mine is a voice that passionately preaches justice and freedom with responsibility; however, not to the exclusion of Jesus. Justice without Jesus will not work for me."[36] She brings accountability to liberation theology by naming responsibility and the need for justice as exemplified by Jesus. Preaching in an urban/inner-city context, Flunder is keenly aware of disparate peoples in her congregation. This she reflects in her sermon when she acknowledges various race, culture, ethnic, gender, nationality, and orientation differences. She examines how we try to dress Jesus in our image, to no avail; Jesus cannot be contained for our purposes. Flunder knows both her congregation ("I preach to a desperate people, who are struggling to make sense of their lives on the margins of society.")

---

36. *www.sfrefuge.org/sermonintro.html.*

and the larger world that is pitted against those in her congregation due to inequities. She manages to preach to both at the same instance.

Her preaching style confirms Henry Mitchell's point of appealing to emotions and thus affirming the truth people know. Flunder is from the Church of God in Christ, a predominantly black Pentecostal denomination, which first influenced her preaching. She writes, "The Pentecostal preaching influence is one where the language is ordered, the lines are metrical and poetic and the sermon is 'sung' in places with the help of the congregation and the musicians. This form of performance art entertained the congregation while driving home the truths in the sermon."[37] True to this description the sermon presented here does almost sing off the page, especially in the closing commands that are written in capital letters. One can almost hear the preacher's sermon as song and the congregation's response. Rather than reasoning with listeners as to Mary's surprise at Jesus' absence from the tomb (as if anyone can offer a reason!), Flunder plows head-on into ways in which we too are like Mary, asking where Jesus has been taken. Like Mary, we can miss where Jesus is when we are looking in places where we expect to find him. In this way, Flunder reaches for our reactions and emotions about this predicament and directs us to a truth we already know: Jesus is free from human constraints, even the constraint of death. It's liberation preaching at its best.

&

The following sermon is an example of a heterosexual ally's preaching. The Reverend Dr. Susan Sumwalt-Patterson preached this sermon at her home congregation in the United Methodist Church and as part of a course in preaching at the Iliff School of Theology in June 2003. This denomination, along with other mainline Protestant denominations, has been debating rules and policies with regard to the lives of gay men and lesbians within their church. In Sumwalt-Patterson's congregation, she reported there was a minimal amount of conversation

---

37. Ibid.

about homosexuality even though the denomination she serves was in a heated battle about the ordination of gay men and lesbians and blessing same-sex unions. As a straight preacher, Reverend Sumwalt-Patterson narrates the often unspoken lives of gays and lesbians in the church.

Sermon:
"ANNIVERSARY"
by Susan Sumwalt-Patterson

Text: Psalm 15:1–2

O Lord, who may abide in your tent?
  Who may dwell on your holy hill?
Those who walk blamelessly, and do what is right
  and speak the truth from their heart.

Harry and Herman had lived in the big brick house on the hill in Willow Bluff for almost half a century. Some assumed that they were bachelor brothers, but the old-timers will tell you that neither of them are natives. Herman came up from Texas in the late '30s to take over the feed mill when Jim Kinnamen died. Harry was from somewhere out East—Delaware or New Jersey. He worked for Herman in the mill, delivering feed and keeping books, until the war came. They tried to enlist together after Pearl Harbor in '41. Herman was accepted and went on to win a Silver Star in the Battle of the Bulge. Harry had a bad eye, so he stayed home and ran the feed mill for Herman. When Herman came home from the war, near the end of '43, business was booming, and he made Harry a full partner. That was when they bought the old Einerson place up on the hill and moved in together. After a few years, folks just came to accept that neither of them was ever going to marry.

Harry and Herman started going to church in '49, just after the addition was built, when Reverend Swingle was pastor. Harry immediately joined the choir. He had a beautiful tenor voice, and when people found out he could sing he became the soloist of choice at most weddings and funerals. Kate Swarmford used to say that Harry had the voice of an angel, and she made her family promise that when she died they would get Harry to sing "The Lord's Prayer" and "K-K-Katie" at her funeral. They kept their promise, and Harry sang both songs just the way she wanted. That was one funeral in Willow Bluff that no one ever forgot. They talk about it to this day.

Herman became active on the church board of trustees. He was often seen over at the church, after work and on Saturday mornings, repairing the roof, painting the trim, or puttering with the furnace. When they installed the new pipe organ in '55, the trustees decided that while there were at it, they might as well renovate the whole sanctuary. Herman headed up the renovation committee. They made him chairman of the trustees the following year, a position he was to hold over thirty years. He had a way of recruiting the right people for a job and organizing them so that things got done in good order.

Their announcement on World Communion Sunday came as a surprise to the congregation and was the source of much puzzlement and consternation in the weeks that followed. Herman stood up during the time for sharing joys and concerns and said, "Harry and I would like to invite everyone to attend our fiftieth anniversary celebration on the nineteenth of November. There will be an announcement in the paper, but we aren't sending any formal invitations. We hope you will be able to come. We have ordered one of those triple-decker cakes from the bakery, and Harry is planning to sing."

The puzzling began as soon as Herman sat down. "Anniversary of what?" Mildred Hersey whispered to her daughter Gyneth, loud enough for half of the congregation to hear. Gyneth shrugged her shoulders and whispered back, "I don't know." No one seemed to know. When the paper came out that Tuesday with Herman and Harry's picture on the front page, the whole town began to buzz. Their announcement simply read, "Herman Fisher and Harry Beechum cordially invite you to attend their fiftieth anniversary celebration on Sunday, November 19, at 2:00 p.m., in the community room at the church."

"I don't understand it," Mildred said to her neighbor, Eunice Criven. "It didn't say fiftieth anniversary of their business or their partnership. You don't suppose they are . . . " She couldn't bring herself to finish the sentence. The very thought was abhorrent to her. "To think that they have been carrying on like that here in Willow Bluff for fifty years. I can tell you right now that I am not going to any anniversary party like that!"

The following Sunday, Herman sat alone in his usual pew in the center of the sanctuary. No one sat near him, and no one greeted him before or after the service. Harry sat with the other tenors in the choir loft, and they spoke to him politely, but there was no joking or laughing as there usually was, and no one said a word about the anniversary celebration. It went on like that for several weeks. People began to wonder why Herman and Harry continued coming to church. There was even some talk about formally asking them to withdraw their memberships.

On the Sunday before the anniversary celebration, the organist, Gena Percy, stood up during joys and concerns and asked the pastor if she could say something to the congregation. The pastor nodded, and Gena stepped out from behind the organ bench, walked over to the center aisle, and with her hands visibly trembling, began to speak. "I want to thank Herman and Harry for what they have done. It has given me the courage to say something that I have wanted to say for a long time. I am a lesbian. I am not ashamed to tell you that now, even though I know that many of you will not understand. I have struggled with who I am for years and years, and after much prayer and the support of several dear friends, I have come to accept all that I am as a gift of God. I don't know why God made me this way.

I have often wished that it could have been otherwise. There have been times when I have wanted to curse God because of the way I have been treated. But I don't feel that way anymore. I think playing the organ in worship has helped. Praising God with this beautiful instrument is the greatest joy of my life. I thank you all for the privilege of serving God as your church organist."

There was no whispering when Gena returned to the bench behind the organ. No one could remember when the church had been so quiet, except perhaps at funerals. It was a holy silence. Everyone who was present knew that he or she had witnessed something extraordinary, and even though they were all shocked and troubled by what Gena had said, they could not bring themselves to condemn her. To have done so would have been to deny what they clearly saw in her face as she spoke: something holy, something that they had no words to describe, but that they knew was of God. Others would condemn her when word got out that Willow Bluff Community Church had a lesbian organist, but they would not. She was one of their own. They had watched her grow up, seen her baptized and confirmed with their own children and grandchildren; they knew her parents and her grandparents, her aunts and uncles, her brothers and her sister. They were all members of the church, too. Whatever else she was, she was their own Gena. Nothing could change that. When one of the newcomers wondered aloud if Gena would be allowed to continue playing the organ, the question was met with a stony silence.

Herman and Harry decorated the community room with crepe paper the following Saturday night. The next day, at 1:45, they stood in their rented tuxedos, waiting to see if anyone would come. Harry said he was willing to bet his next Social Security check that they would be eating freezer-burnt anniversary cake for several months. But by 2:15 the room was full and people were still coming. After they had opened their gifts, and Herman had made a little speech thanking everyone for coming and saying the usual things about what a blessing it was to have so many faithful friends, Harry announced that he had a song he would like to share. He walked over to the piano, where Gena was already seated, and after she played the introduction, he smiled at Herman and began to sing in his sweet tenor voice:

> For all the years, these friends and these blessings,
> We give you all praise mighty God.
> For trials, temptations, and hardships endured,
> We thank you, O Lord, our salvation.
> For this holy union of sinners forgiven,
> Redeemed, transformed, sanctified;
> For grace all sufficient, sustaining, maintaining
> Our love all these years, thank you, God.[38]

When the singing finished, guests began to thank Harry and Herman for such a lovely party, and some were heard to offer "Congratulations" on their anniversary. After enjoying cake and talking some more, guests began to leave and Harry, Herman, and Gena were left in the community room with the aftermath of a party. However, what they knew in their hearts was the beginning of a new era in their church life and in their lives as well. Something else had been celebrated here on this day — God's amazing love that redeems and restores relationships. The tent — God's dwelling place — is both larger than any of us could imagine and as near as our own hearts flung wide open. Amen.

Analysis

When a straight preacher tells a story like this in his or her sermon, it is his or her coming out too. A straight preacher can say things

---

38. John E. Sumwalt, *Lectionary Stories: Cycle C, 40 Tellable Tales for Preaching* (Lima: C.S.S. Publications, 1991). Music by Kerri Sherwood, "Anniversary," First United Methodist Church, Kenosha, Wisconsin, CSS Publishing Company, Inc. Lima, Ohio, and words by John Sumwalt.

to a congregation that a homosexual preacher cannot without serious repercussions. When I was told not to preach about "it" anymore in my church, I realized that as out gay and lesbian preachers we embodied the very thing people were afraid might split their church, encroach on their values, hurt their children, or tarnish their image. It comes back to the images of God that people have collected through sermons and their life experiences, and what they have or have not been taught about sexuality. When all of these coalesce in the preacher, it makes it difficult for people to hear. In this sermon, a straight preacher narrates life in another church with characters who come out in both subtle and bold ways. Each character comes to his or her own truth in his or her own time and tells it when she or he is ready. When their congregation ostracized Harry and Herman, Gena stepped forward and spoke up. She names clearly who she is — a lesbian — who had been invisible to them up to that time. Like Esther, Gena comes out from a position of privilege within the community,

> For if you keep silence at such a time as this, relief and deliverance will rise for the Jews from another quarter, but you and your father's family will perish. Who knows? Perhaps you have come to royal dignity for just such a time as this. (Esther 4:14)

Since Gena was one of "them," the congregation could not reject her as they were doing with Harry and Herman. Gena's coming out invited the congregation to reconsider their beliefs and prejudices toward homosexuals. In so doing, it freed them from their fears, and they celebrated with Harry and Herman. The listener can imagine that the congregation had recovered something they did not even know they had lost.

This sermon is also an excellent example of the inductive method of preaching. There is no persuasion or deductive teaching about the Scripture. The message of the Scripture is overheard in the story. Particularly when dealing with sensitive subject matters like homosexuality, it is very useful for preachers to employ a method that delivers a new hearing without telling the congregation exactly what to believe. Retired preaching professor from the Candler School of Theology, Fred Craddock placed the listener at the center of preaching and gave the listener the privacy and right to determine meaning. Craddock based his inductive method on giving the listener credit for his or her ability to understand the gospel: "For the listener, there is in the indirect method complete respect. The listener is respected for what is already known."[39] Noting that people respond by overhearing a situation rather than being told directly, Craddock believed this method was more effective for transformation in preaching the gospel.[40] This sermon has a narrative, storylike quality that is easier on the listener's ear.

Theologically, this sermon errs on the side of grace rather than judgment, as does Thomas Troeger's sermon in chapter 2. The grace implies that human beings, in this case the church family, were able to participate in a redemptive way in the lives of Herman and Harry by celebrating their years of love together with them. Theologically, grace, in this story, was operative in liberating people from their fear of gay or lesbian people and restoring relationships as God sees them rather than with human distortions. However, not just heterosexuals but all people exist with some level of fear in their lives, which prevents all of us from experiencing the fullness of life. Fear diminishes us. Love restores us.

Scripturally, the sermon answers the psalmist's question, "O Lord, Who may abide in your tent?" As the preacher tells about the lives of Harry, Herman, and Gena, she describes them as those who are blameless, who do what is right, and who speak the truth from their heart, paralleling the psalmist's writings. Interweaving the lives of lesbians and gay men with the righteous lives in the Bible can free us from thinking only heterosexuals are in the Bible. By allowing their personal lives to be visible, Gena, Harry, and Herman take the congregation

---

39. Fred Craddock, *Overhearing the Gospel* (St. Louis: Chalice Press, 2002), 78.
40. Ibid., 91.

to a new place; they bring the congregation to a new awareness about God's creation and love for everyone.

The preacher in this sermon got out of the way and did not try to confront the listeners with her truth or even a specific truth. She kept the psalmist's questions about who may abide in the temple or dwell on the holy hill in tension with the congregation's unfolding story — who was allowed in their congregation. In the story, just as the congregants are about to turn their backs on Harry and Herman, Gena speaks up. Through imagination and biblical interpretation, the truth of God is made alive and available to the hearers.

Preaching comes out when the preacher is aware of and in touch with the sacredness of his or her sexuality in whole body preaching. Speaking truth through personality includes the words we preach and the experience of being in our body. Thus a lesbian and gay homiletic will be centered in the biblical text and the text of our body, ours and the congregation's, and theological reflection on who God is for us and who we are for God in that particular time and place. The four tasks of preaching illuminated by Buber's I-Thou theology give definition to this homiletic that will draw attention to the queer God in our midst. Whether through narrative, expository, deductive, inductive, literary, or postmodern preaching, what becomes clear in a lesbian and gay homiletic is that preaching is not a heterosexual activity. LGBT clergy and their allies preach and when they do, God comes out! Meeting this queer God is the subject of the next chapter.

Chapter 6

God Comes Out

When an out lesbian, gay, or bisexual clergyperson preaches, God comes out of heterosexism. The closet door opens to reveal in that clergyperson made in the image of God something about God's nature. It opens on the hidden face of a gay God who longs to be welcomed into full communion. As is true with a person of color or a woman who preaches, color and gender reveal something about the nature of God. But it is not only the person, or the body, but the message which this person brings in the sermon that reveals something of the person and therefore of God. His or her sexuality is not the point of the sermon, yet all of a preacher's personhood or identity plays a central role in the experience of preaching, both for the preacher and for the hearers — and that includes their sexuality.

That being the case, this chapter explores the idea of God coming out as a sexual minority from the perspective of one within that group. Queering God — thinking about God as a same-gender-loving Creator — gives us an image to work with in developing a lesbian and gay homiletical method. Like traveling to a new place, this excursion will take us down various streets where lesbians and gay men are practicing a spiritual life and faith in Christ. Some of them are in the church, some in the academy, some in lesbian and gay community events, some in welcoming churches, and some outside the traditional Christian church. Wherever they are, they are all contributing to the process of outing God.

How we think about, how we imagine, and how we name God have preoccupied us humans for centuries. And our response has changed with time and experience. The struggle to name or describe God is important for each generation as we learn, grow, and understand in order to deepen our relationship with God. A majority of the time it is the trained theologians, ministers, and priests who are in the business of defining God for the collective people. It is they who have typically been seen as having access to the power of naming for others.

Most of this imagery or naming of God over the centuries has excluded descriptions of sexuality. As the Christian church moved from being a disorganized collection of Jesus followers into the established state religion, women were excluded from leadership positions. The men in charge apparently had difficulty with sexuality, for they saw it as a necessary evil. Sex was something that had to be done to further the species, but not for enjoyment or pleasure. The God of sex was repressed and sex was seen as a sin, and women vilified as the temptress, the seducer, the worldlier, and curiously the weaker, and therefore the ones to be kept outside the inner sanctum of religion and out of positions of power.

Though we are all sexual human beings, Christianity has tended not to validate and hold in high esteem sexual experiences. So it is hardly surprising that it has also been reluctant to connect sexual experience in an affirming way with a person's experience of God. Left to determine how God fits into this intimate and yet powerful place in our lives, we cannot do so, and so we dismiss our sexuality and sexual expression as something dirty or bad but certainly outside of our understanding of religious experience.

With the sexual revolution and now the coming out of lesbians and gay men in the church, conversation about sexuality and God has come out of the closet. An analysis of sexual constructions within the LGBT/queer Christian community is an invitation to sexual honesty for all. If the church were a safe place for honesty, we might see the discussion of sexuality as a means to our connection with God as a path to God rather than away from God. We might see our erotic (eros) longing for reunion or connection as a good and wholesome part of our humanity, something worthy of recognition, honor, and celebration rather than as a disconnection or sin. If we did this, we

would understand that it is the way we manage this erotic desire —
and not the desire itself (whether for same- or other-sex persons) —
that is of more consequence. God's coming out in terms of sexuality
is indeed a major move in Christianity.

Such a coming out is much broader than simply naming God as
male or female, gay or straight or lesbian, and so on. When speaking
about God, metaphors and models in our postmodern scientific context are increasingly impersonal and less anthropocentric. In spite of
our enlightened views that have called for a diversity of names for
God, there is still a need for personal and human images of God. One
reason for this need is because we are embodied beings and we tend
to create God in our own image since it is the one we know best.
Second, the incarnation of God into our world through Jesus Christ
and the Spirit's presence in our lives invites us into relationship with
God and others. To image or name God in ways that are mechani-
cal or technological does not reflect this relationship of intimacy with
the Creator. In the biblical world, the primary way God is described
is in relationship with creation, specifically humanity. The relationship begins in the first chapter of Genesis where humanity is made in
the image of God, and it continues throughout the course of human
history.

Bring Many Names for God

The Bible is replete with humans in relationship with one another and
with their Creator. How we portray these relationships in our sermons
reveals the extent of our I-Thou relational theology and methodology: How diverse are our images? Do our images of God in sermons
reflect the diversity of scriptural images of mother hen and warrior
and woman in labor and Creator, or do we repeat the familiar ones of
father and king?

A closer study in the Hebrew Scriptures particularly reveals that
God is depicted as a multidimensional character with more than one
identity. Author Jack Miles, in his book *God: A Biography*, suggests that

God is perhaps one character among other characters in the Hebrew Scriptures, like Moses, Miriam, and Joseph. God appears in Genesis 1–4 as benevolent Creator of the universe, creating the world, naming the creatures, and setting aside a day for rest. God urges human creation: "Be fruitful and multiply" (Genesis 1:28). Once Adam and Eve are constructed and have eaten the fruit, it is God who becomes a "Seamstress," sewing clothes for them to wear. It is this same God who then turns into an angry "Destroyer" (Genesis 4–11), when Cain kills Abel, and then sends the Flood (Genesis 9). Miles sees God as a character developing alongside the story itself.[1] Rather than seeing God as existing outside of (removed from or above) the biblical text, Miles's approach allows room for imagination and suggests an infinitely complex God involved in the lives and events narrated — hence the wonderful diversity of images of God in the biblical texts, including Creator, Punisher, Mother Hen, Lawgiver, Coach, Judge, Jury, Lawyer, Friend, Covenant Maker, Personal Confidant, Executioner, Warrior, Deliverer, Shepherd, Comforter, and Destroyer.

Do our sermons reflect this diversity of images for God? If so, might the congregation be open to change when it occurs in pastoral leadership? When another preacher enters the pulpit who is not a heterosexual, married male, it is difficult to make such a transition. Over time, the images of God we hear in sermons solidify a particular aspect or image of God, much as, of course, do images of men and women and children, too. Not only do sermons carry multiple images, but so does the preacher's identity — whether she or he be black or brown, yellow or white, gay or straight, transgender or bisexual, female or male. And so we bring the image of God into play with the reality of LGBT lives and ask the question, "Then what would a lesbian or gay God look and act like?"

---

1. Jack Miles, *God: A Biography* (New York: Alfred A. Knopf, 1995), 28–35.

Divine Gayness

Can gay be one of these aspects of the divine? What would a lesbian God look like? How might the queer community see God in their image? How would a gay God further the mission of the church? Let us imagine for a moment what it would be like if God or an aspect of God came out. Like the majority of gay people, God would suffer rejection from family and friends (though some lesbians and gay men have a positive coming out experience). God would probably lose some of those beloved people in the coming out process and wonder why. God would have to go in search of support and help from others who have experienced a similar reaction. God, I imagine, would find other friends and form new relationships. God would experience betrayal, hopelessness, pain, and fear of being beaten or killed. At some time, God might become angry and join an organization like ACT-UP (AIDS Coalition to Unleash Power). God would march in pride parades and go to rallies and hearings to support equal rights for all sexual minorities. God would dress in drag. God would buy a rainbow bumper sticker and self-identify as part of the rainbow tribe. God would celebrate with others coming out and ease the pain or sorrow when needed. As every lesbian or gay man has had to consider for her or himself, God would have to ask, "What are the risks of my God coming out?" Of course, this exercise is purely to stretch the imagination and bring two contradictory worlds together, but it is a crucial step out of oppression to imagine God in drag, or Jesus as a homosexual, or a lesbian Holy Spirit. This is how the LGBT community of faith needs to reflect on God and their creation in the image of God.

Wondering theologically about what it would mean for God to come out, I think of the in-vogue expression from and title of a popular cable show, "Queer Eye for the Straight Guy."[2] The show brings five gay men into a straight man's life to do a complete makeover of him — his

---

2. Cable show: *Queer Eye for the Straight Guy*. Used irreverently to make a point about the necessity of doing queer theology.

clothes, home, hair, habits — so he is more attractive. This is a comical approach to God and yet touches on the need for theology that reflects the LGBT Christian community. "Queer eye for the straight God" is what I mean by "queering" God; it is to challenge the prevailing heterosexual assumptions about the One we call Maker of All. For us, as queer Christian theologians, to make over our straight God will require creativity. It will stretch the imagination. It will be necessary to suspend judgment and listen.

Personal Approach

In an effort to reflect upon God from the vantage point of the lesbian and gay community, I will describe experiences at primarily LGBT events. I do not speak for the entire community, or for any one particular lesbian or gay man. Also, there are those who do not identify with the cultural movement of "gay liberation" and therefore, quite possibly, would think my descriptions unnecessary in this effort. As an author, trying to describe accurately a community that covers upward of 10 percent of the entire population of the world is impossible. Let me offer my limited knowledge of and experience within the gay and lesbian movement. Local and national LGBT events include Gay Pride Parades in remembrance of the Stonewall riots, the 1993 March on Washington for equal rights for the LGBT population; the Gay Games (which began in 1982 and have been held every four years as both athletic and cultural events in major cities around the world), and the AIDS Quilt on display at the Washington Mall in D.C. and various other cities.

At each of these large gatherings of LGBT people and straight allies, I have witnessed three reoccurring aspects of the community: an abundance of color, joy, and diversity. The rainbow flag (red, orange, yellow, green, blue, purple) was adopted during the gay liberation movement as a banner of welcome, inclusion, and creativity, all of which abound in the LGBT community. Perhaps the rainbow flag was adopted because lesbians and gay men were looking for a safe place, like the one popularized in the song "Somewhere over the Rainbow." This song from *The Wizard of Oz* and its singer/actress Judy Garland became icons of hope primarily for gay men after the Stonewall riots. The rainbow put in the sky by God, as a reminder that the earth and its inhabitants would never be destroyed again (Genesis 9), also serves as a symbol of hope and promise. To this day, rainbow colors appear on flags, bumper stickers, and pendants to symbolize and identify with the LGBT community. The 1994 Gay Pride Parade in New York City coincided with the start of the Gay Games with a fabric rainbow flag three miles long carried by thousands of people down main streets. This event illustrates the number, strength, and beauty of the LGBT movement.

The joy and camaraderie at such events is powerful. These are places where LGBT folk, young and old, can find each other, and can be free, finally, to be who they are and celebrate something that they usually have to keep hidden. Imagine your life lived in two ways, one for approval and the other for your deep sense of self. Think of living in the shadows or alleys or doorways or closets most days of your life. And then imagine a place where you can bring yourself into the light, into community with others, into full view and to be appreciated, known, and seen for who you are. I know from experience that it is truly amazing. At the 1993 March on Washington we rode the long escalators up from the underground subways into daylight and joined thousands of others celebrating their full selves. This experience reminded me of an image from a movie that same year, *Schindler's List*. This black-and-white movie recounts how Nazi businessman Oskar Schindler helped eleven hundred Polish Jews escape the death camps.[3] At the end of this gritty and intense movie, the survivors come walking toward the viewer, at last being set free, and as they do, they come from black-and-white into full color. The colors symbolize their freedom and new life after the Holocaust. Granted, the typical experience of sexual minorities in the United States is nothing like

---

3. *Schindler's List* (1993), Steven Spielberg, director, Universal Studios.

that of death camps, yet perhaps it is a fitting image both for coming out of the closet and riding escalators to a pride parade. From living in the shadows of our closets, our lives go from black-and-white to technicolor as we venture out into the world beyond our closets.

As for the diversity at such events, one can let the imagination run with the wind: every color, race, nationality, religious expression can be found here — a rainbow of colors in dress and flags, leather groups, dykes on bikes, fairies, families with children, grandparents, drag queens and kings, cross dressers, male strippers, political activists, square dancers, peaceniks and youth groups, and so on. The following obituary from the *Denver Post* describes the difference one straight man sees between himself and his gay brother.

> The deceased studied hairdressing. He began work at the May Co. He was a Christian, but embraced much of Buddhism, his brother said. He loved the theatre and fine dining, collected Asian art and Russian lacquer boxes and decorated at least three Christmas trees in his home each year. To the end, "he believed in Santa Claus, unicorns, fairies and all things good," his brother said. Robert laughed when he talked about how close he and his brother were despite their differences. "I am straight and see muted colors. My brother was gay and saw the world in Technicolor. Wherever he found it wanting, he was happy to supply a splash of color, a fawn of feathers, and a string of rhinestones."[4]

This comparison of muted colors with technicolor is a vivid description of what some gay men offer the world around them. Gay men are as notorious for their flamboyant style, design, color, and decorating capacities as lesbians are for their "handy-man" ability with tools or bookish ways. These are stereotypical generalizations, yet they live in the consciousness of society, for ill or good.

Certainly some characteristic descriptors and attributes are transferred in our preaching by out lesbian and gay clergy. Would we say

---

4. *Denver Post*, May 7, 2006.

our preaching is more colorful? Could we offer a rainbow God that rescues people from their black-and-white lives? If we could take a poll of listeners who, over time, have heard out lesbian and gay clergy preach, what might their image of God be?

A study of attributes of straight preachers versus lesbian and gay preachers would, I imagine, be quite revealing. In 1980, after women clergy numbers increased and we preached with greater frequency, a study by the College of Preachers in Washington D.C. revealed perceived gender differences in the sermons of male and female preachers.[5] Men's preaching was described using more favorable adjectives such as intellectual, confident, and organized while women's preaching was perceived to be the weaker (emotional, too personal, hesitant). Given the struggle to attain the position of preacher, women had struggled with self-esteem and competency issues. When the same survey was administered in 1994 when female preachers had greater experience and exposure in pulpits, the respondents perceived women's preaching skills to "register a stronger feeling response," being overall more positive.[6] Perhaps a similar study of lesbian and gay preachers versus straight preachers now and in fifteen years would yield parallel gains in acceptance and a uniqueness we offer in preaching. Through my research and experience, I venture three adjectives descriptive of preaching by out lesbian and gay clergy: bold, unique, and colorful.

Coming Out as Revelation

My sense that God comes out through out lesbian and gay preachers, both in their being and in their sermons, was developed prior to reading Chris Glaser's book *Coming Out as Sacrament*. He also has a chapter titled "God Comes Out," in which he explores how God

---

5. O. C. Edwards Jr., *A History of Preaching* (Nashville: Abingdon Press, 2004), 752.

6. Ibid., 753.

reveals Godself through the Scriptures. This idea of "God comes out" enters the collection of lesbian and gay writings through Glaser's work. The chapter discusses the difficulty in naming God. Sensitive to labels given to LGBT persons, Glaser reminds his readers that the second and third commandments convey God's concern for those who would either make an idol of his name or misuse it (Exodus 20:4–7). Glaser sees God's process of coming out in theological terms of revelation and argues that the Bible is the source for this "coming out." To illustrate places of revelation in the Bible, Glaser writes:

> The biblical writers saw God revealed in: the creation of the cosmos; the rainbow promise after the flood; a burning bush in Egyptian wilderness; thunder and lightning on Mount Sinai; a still small voice to Elijah on Mount Horeb; a stranger in a fiery furnace with Shadrach, Meshach, and Abednego; a defender of the marginalized; a Deity for all nations; a conception of Mary; and a compassionate rabbi and healer named Jesus.[7]

After noting these revelations, Glaser writes of this truth in a very bold way: "we reveal the glory of sexuality itself, a divinely created and graciously given glory that the church has also veiled, demanding that we veil our faces because we have seen in our sexuality the glory of God."[8] Glaser makes a strong point here about lesbians and gay men in our discovery of our sexual connections with another. But of course, he is not the first to write about sexual connections with another human being compared with our relationship to the divine. There is a whole body of writings from within the Christian church that reflect this very aspect, though these writings are seldom referred to because they deal with the still rather taboo subject of sexuality.

---

7. Chris Glaser, *Coming Out as Sacrament* (Louisville: Westminster John Knox Press, 1992), 85.
   8. Ibid., 91.

Mystical Approaches

The mystics of the thirteenth and fourteenth centuries wrote about God in ways that are similar to sexual and intimate experiences with another human being. Reading church history, the mystics are given a place, but their writings did not seem to change the overall attitudes toward sexuality. A few excerpts from their writings give a glimpse into their world. Even though taken out of context, these lines compare God with a human lover:

> *English mystic Julian of Norwich* (1342–1416): "God wants to be thought of as our lover. That is to say, the love of God makes such a unity in us that when we see this unity no one is able to separate oneself from another."[9]

> *German mystic Mechtild of Magdeburg* (1210–83): "O you flowing God in your love! O you burning God in your desire! O you melting God in the union with your beloved! O you resting God on my breasts! Without you I cannot exist."[10]

> *German mystic Meister Eckhart* (1260–1327): "If therefore I am changed into God and He makes me one with Himself, then, by the living God, there is no distinction between us.... By knowing God I take him to myself. By loving God, I penetrate him."[11]

Scholarly Approaches

In current academic circles, there are some hints of God, Jesus or Christ, the Spirit, the Trinity, and other aspects of Christianity as perceived from an LGBT perspective. Most writings focus on Jesus from a gay perspective, as does author Theodore W. Jennings in his

---

9. Brendan Doyle, *Meditations of Julian of Norwich* (Santa Fe: Bear and Company, 1983), 113.

10. Mechtild of Magdeburg, *The Flowing Light of the Godhead*, trans. Frank Tobin (Mahwah, NJ: Paulist Press, 1998), 1:17, 19.

11. Meister Eckhart, *Meister Eckhart*, trans. R. B. Blakney (New York: Harper & Brothers, 1941), 181–82.

book *The Man Jesus Loved* by asking the question, "Was Jesus Gay?"[12] Another author, Robert Goss, in his book *Queering Christ* looks at the historical role of Jesus through the church as he wrestles with what Christology looks like from a gay man's perspective. As Goss "queers" Christ, he elaborates on what he thinks LGBT Christians bring to the table:

> The theological task of queer theologies will continue to be determining the implications of God's revelation through a community primarily consisting of queer Christians and determining what this means for life and ministry to the mainline churches and the world. Queer theologies espouse an ecumenical vision of community, doctrine, human sexuality, prophetic ministry, and human liberation.[13]

What Goss outlines here is a tall order for the queer community, as small as it is in the Christian church. The work of creating an ecumenical vision of community, doctrine, human sexuality, prophetic ministry, and human liberation cannot be done without the support and assistance of straight allies in positions of power, able to influence construction of such writings and proclamation. As this work is done alongside the coming out of queer Christians within local churches, a new sexual ethic will develop that will be liberating for heterosexuals as well.

We in the gay community are accused quite often of talking too much about sex. It is true, we do. Discovering our sexuality is both a source of pain and one of pleasure. Because we have discovered what is integral to our being that is different from the majority, we need to talk about it as we integrate it into our lives and our spirituality. Like Glaser said, we have "seen in our sexuality the glory of God" and are not afraid to tell others. There is an excitement about sex that is hard

---

12. Theodore W. Jennings Jr., *The Man Jesus Loved: Homoerotic Narratives from the New Testament* (Cleveland: Pilgrim Press, 2003), 233.

13. Robert Goss, *Queering Christ* (Cleveland: Pilgrim Press, 2002), 256.

to contain. Sex talk among heterosexual Christians is but a whisper. Misplaced expectations about what sex is supposed to be like in any marriage causes more pain than joy. Being able to talk frankly without fear and receive support and insight into one's sexual life is liberating. The mind is our most powerful sex organ, and it operates in ways we do not always understand. Being able to talk about one's passion or fantasies with a trusted friend or within one's faith community could demystify our sexual desires and bring them into play as a source of goodness and grace provided by God.

One attempt at a new Christian sex ethic from a straight perspective is *Lily among the Thorns: Imaging a New Christian Sexuality* by Miguel A. De La Torre.[14] De La Torre takes the command in Genesis 1:28, "Be fruitful and multiply," to mean God declared sex good and encouraged humans to engage in it. Extracting this command before the traditional teachings against sex based on Adam and Eve and the serpent's dialogue, De La Torre claims the erotic life as pleasurable as well as necessary for the continuation of the human species. However, this pro-sex God of De La Torre's work fails to address same-gender sexual practice from the beginning of his ethic. It also comes dangerously close to the argument used against same-sex love — that our love is not procreative in the sense of producing offspring. I would counter that sex is procreative regardless of whether it bears children because it immerses us in our desire and longing, which is ultimately union and reunion with our Maker. The Song of Songs from the Bible might be a more solid foundation for building a new sexual ethic that includes all from the beginning and is not directed toward procreation.

Another scholar and theologian whose work is primarily being read in academic circles is Marcella Althaus-Reid, professor of systematic theology and Christian ethics at the University of Edinburgh, Scotland. Althaus-Reid is pushing traditional theology to examine its heterosexism in order to see more clearly the queer God. At the same

---

14. Miguel De La Torre, *Lily among the Thorns: Imaging a New Christian Sexuality* (San Francisco: Jossey-Bass, 2007), 2.

time she is critiquing liberation theology as insufficient for this task. She is creating theological discourse about the "queer" God in her second book:

> *The Queer God* is a book about the re-discovery of God outside the heterosexual ideology which has been prevalent in the history of Christianity and theology. In order to do that, it is necessary to facilitate the coming out of the closet of God by a process of theological queering. By theological queering, we mean the deliberate questioning of heterosexual experience and thinking which has shaped our understanding of theology, the role of the theologian and hermeneutics. It is from there that not only do we rediscover the face of the Queer God, but also find our relationship with God challenged and see emerging new reflections on holiness and on Christianity.[15]

Through the lives of those economically marginalized and those who are sexual minorities, Althaus-Reid produces an image of the queer God that is radical in nature. Her work unzips the presence of sexuality in traditional Christian thought. For instance, in her "queer theology" she suggests that one must examine the sexual relationships in the Trinity. The intimacy of the three in relationship creates the Trinity — God, Jesus, and Spirit — one body, one God, in three persons. What can we say about bodies — human bodies and divine bodies — that illuminate our understanding of relationship to God, Jesus, and the Spirit? Three human bodies together sexually might suggest an orgy or at least multiple partners in relationship. Essentially, queer theology searches every aspect of the Divine and our theological presuppositions with eyes, ears, lips, hands, and nose toward sexual energy and relationship. Althaus-Reid's theological work joins that of others outing God in the academic realm.

---

15. Marcella Althaus-Reid, *The Queer God* (London and New York: Routledge, 2003), 2–3.

Congregational Approaches

Drawing on the "I-Thou" relational model outlined earlier, there are three actions congregations can take to imagine God coming out as a gay God. The first is to ask the question, "What would a gay God look like?" Second, Christians in the LGBT community need to answer this query. Third, straight preachers, teachers, theologians, and church folk need to listen. While this is primarily an exercise in imaginative thinking and respectful listening, there are excellent denominational resources to assist groups that desire such conversation.[16]

Recent scholarship has done just this — listened to the lives of gay and lesbian clergy — through interviews with couples who are both committed to ordained ministry and to a life of holiness with a partner of the same sex.[17] Using Dietrich Bonhoeffer's instructive words, "We should listen with the ears of God that we may speak the word of God," author Jeffrey Heskins yields to this maxim by listening before speaking. Out of this exercise, our image of God will include lesbian, gay, bisexual, transgender, and queer aspects of the divine. Asking "What does a gay God look like?" raises the question of coming out and subsequently pushes theological discourse beyond surface debates about homosexuality as sinful. Surely, conversations such as this are taking place in welcoming churches already.

Welcoming Church Approaches

While struggling for justice in mainline churches through policy changes, LGBT Christians have formed the Welcoming Church movement as described earlier in this work. One purpose of this association of churches and members is to identify with one another for general

---

16. See, for example, resources provided by the United Church of Christ, the Unitarian Universalists, the Episcopal Church, the Presbyterian Church (USA), and other churches in the Welcoming Churches movement.

17. Jeffrey Heskins, *Face-to-Face: Gay and Lesbian Clergy on Holiness and Life Together* (Grand Rapids: Wm. Eerdmans, 2006).

support and collegiality. At the two major conferences, our opportunities for worship, connection, and mutual direction in ministry enabled us to do our own theological work. Gaining insights and creating a supportive network, we were able to return to ministry within mainline denominations.

In the closing worship service for the Witness Our Welcome Conference in 2003, Rev. Troy Perry, founder of the Universal Fellowship Metropolitan Community Church, walked down the aisle at the end of the procession.[18] Before him had gone a long line of participants in the worship service who were waving rainbow banners, dancing, singing, and carrying the bread and wine jugs, as we sang the opening hymn. Rev. Perry was wearing beautiful red and white liturgical vestments and carrying a large plate of fruit. Highly visible on the fruit plate was a pineapple, an ancient sign for "welcome" or "hospitality." It was so moving to see this symbol used in such a creative way by a man who has made it his life mission to create a safe, sacred sanctuary for thousands and thousands of lesbians, gays, bisexuals, transgender people, and queer people. I thought how brave he was to start a gay church in 1968, and how many lives the MCC has literally and spiritually saved by their presence. He placed the fruit plate on the communion table along with the bread and wine. There on the heavenly banquet table a pineapple sat, sending us a message of "welcome" in God's realm. This welcoming image of God as represented in the pineapple on the communion table represents hope for all LGBT Christians seeking inclusion.

The understanding and experience of being welcomed at the table is powerful for those who have been rejected by family, friends, and the church because of their sexual orientation. There is a profound gladness and joy of coming home to God experienced in services

---

18. Witness Our Welcome is a triennial conference sponsored by the Welcoming Church movement. The first was in 2000 in Peoria, Illinois, and the 2003 conference was in Philadelphia. Approximately seven hundred to eight hundred Christians from the LGBTQ community attended.

where there is visibility by LGBT members. This spirited energy and excitement is a gift the LGBT community has to bring the church.

Another Approach

There are many authors outside of the mainline denominations writing about their experience of being lesbian or gay and their spiritual lives. Theirs is important work for what we can glean from the culture's perception about same-gender love and God. Some are former ministers, and in the case of gay author Toby Johnson a former monk. He names the gay perspective as revolutionary in his book *Gay Perspective*. Johnson describes a unique and life-giving picture of spirituality from a homosexual's view, as opposed to old-time religion or mainline denominations of superstition, fear, and exclusion. He includes chapters on how our homosexuality tells us things about life, sex, religion, the church, God, and the world, and in so doing he weaves a narrative about all the ways gay people can help society transcend ignorance and embrace love and compassion.

Johnson explains that by living outside typical gender norms, gay people are able to see across boundaries of gender and gain access to a less dualistic outlook on the nature of life. Because of this, gay people are attuned to the needs of a rapidly evolving society in which quick and nimble thinking is in demand and gender equality is rapidly becoming an expected norm. Yet all the while traditional religions are beset with internal conflicts, exposing inherent contradictions between organized religion and the true nature of God. For Johnson, being homosexual has a purpose in the world at this particular time: "Our homosexuality is bigger than we are; it transcends our individual existence. It is a reality we participate in, a quality of God manifesting itself in the world. Studying our experience of homosexuality reveals why we're here at this particular moment in history and how playing these particular roles serves the evolution of consciousness."[19]

19. Toby Johnson, *Gay Perspective: Things Our Homosexuality Tells Us about the Nature of God and the Universe* (Los Angeles: Alyson, 2003), 37.

Johnson's book, among others, is contributing to a growing body of spiritual resources within the larger LGBT community. These contributions offer honest and faithful theological work about who God is for LGBT people, even if it is not currently recognized by mainline churches. LGBT people not currently in churches are seeking spiritual nourishment, and these books fill that need. Though once on a spiritual path, seekers long for a spiritual home or "community" such as a church, but finding that place and the welcome is arduous.

Homiletical Approaches

The image of a God who comes out — a queer God — in our sermons will be challenging to say the least. With exegesis of the Bible and the congregation, imagination will be an important tool in sermon writing. Thinking theologically about what a gay God looks like will call forth our most creative minds. Homileticians Thomas Troeger and Paul Wilson speak of finding "imagination at the juncture of human spirit and Holy Spirit, channeling divine creativity through human creativity to fashion new visions of the kingdom."[20] For a lesbian and gay homiletic, imagination will be a useful device for envisioning a world of inclusion in God's realm. All preaching needs to be imaginative and visionary with textual and contextual engagement to lift us out of a sedentary position into the world of service; from the dead end of discussion about sexual orientation to the light of movement, dance, music, and celebration at God's banquet table.

Imaginative preaching is also important in a time of crisis because it helps us speak with pastoral sensitivity and insight to hurting and confused people — not to suggest that God's coming out or the image of a gay God will create a crisis, but rather to acknowledge that the

20. Cited in Don M. Wardlaw, "Homiletics and Preaching in North America," *Concise Encyclopedia of Preaching,* ed. William H. Willimon and Richard Lischer (Louisville: Westminster John Knox Press, 1995), 250.

church is already in crisis over sexuality. With that particular awareness, Joseph Jeter's book *Crisis Preaching* is a guide through turmoil in
the church. It gives insight in ways to respond to a crisis by taking a
particular look at the situation. To begin with, Jeter splits crises into
two categories: external and internal. The external or public crisis
is concerned with events in our society or nation such as the Okla-
homa City bombing, the Columbine High School shootings, and the
events of September 11, 2001. External crises also include natural
disasters: famine, hurricanes, earthquakes, floods, and fires. Certainly,
these events affect the congregation, sometimes directly, but always in
the psyche of the people. Internal church crisis refers, for example, to
a death of a family in the congregation, a murder of a member, money
mismanagement, or firing a minister. A subcategory within internal
church crises is the minister who is in personal crisis due to illness,
personal tragedy, loss of faith, coming out, ethical or sexual miscon-
duct, or divorce. While helpful in sorting out different kinds of crises
a church may face, Jeter's writing is particularly important in noting
that all these theological concerns are of one nature: theodicy — the
question of "Is God?"[21] People want to know if God "is" when a crisis
has occurred. When there is a traumatic natural or personal crisis,
people naturally ask questions about God's presence, the primary one
being the most foundational: "Is God?" This question can be asked
or stated several different ways: "Where is God?" "Why did God let
this happen?" "If this happened, then there isn't a God." The concerns raised in a crisis have to do with understanding and deciding
how to respond. *Understanding* has to do with *theology*, and deciding
what to do in response has to do with *ethics*. It is the *why* and *what*
of a given situation that provide clues for our preaching. Perhaps the
church's crisis about sexuality is, in part, due to our relationship to
our image of God.

---

21. Joseph R. Jeter Jr., *Crisis Preaching: Personal and Public* (Nashville: Abingdon
Press, 1998), 25.

Returning to Jeter's work, one strategy he suggests for preaching in a crisis is the use of poetic questions — symbolic or metaphoric ways of expressing the depths of meaning or misery. Troeger's sermon in chapter 2 is an excellent example of using poetic and metaphorical imagery as a way to talk about God in the midst of a human tragedy. Thinking of God as Weaser offers a new image of God in the much-needed despair over Shepard's death. Weaser as God is totally new and unexpected. For people mourning the murder of a gay man, having God revealed in a different image than "the father" or "Savior" or "omnipotent ruler" helped bring the world of LGBT and the church closer. My sermon "Wheat or Weeds?" (chapter 3) is similar in its use of wheat and weeds as metaphors for people in all their humanity. In the biblical world of Scripture, Jesus often used familiar symbols — yeast, seeds, soil, grapes, trees, birds — to convey the message without speaking directly to the issue. Parables like wheat and weeds give rise to greater meaning than frank and direct speech.

ॐ

The following two sermons are by out lesbian and gay clergy. Using imagination and biblical imagery, they create a coming out for God. Their sermons bring Scripture into play with the idea of a lesbian or gay God.

The first sermon, "Swish,"[22] is by Rev. Dr. Janie Adams Spahr, minister of That All May Freely Serve. This sermon was preached at the Downtown United Presbyterian Church, Rochester, New York, on July 14, 2002. Initially this church called Spahr to be one of its co-pastors. When the Permanent Judicial Committee of the Presbyterian Church (USA) voted to rescind her call, Downtown United Presbyterian Church created a unique position. The church called her as an evangelist, a position for which the same ordination rules did not apply as for a co-pastor. She has served in this position since 1993.

---

22. Janie Adams Spahr, "SWISH," *www.tamfs.org*.

Sermon:
"SWISH"

by Janie Adams Spahr

Texts: Proverbs 8:1–9; Matthew 15:15–20

Basketball! It is the "swish" sound of the basketball through the net I think that first stirred inside me. Swish — and I was hooked on basketball. As a freshman in high school I would sneak over to the gym in the evening and shoot baskets. There were some nights, the moments the ball left my hand I knew it would swish into the net — and in she sank. From dribbling to hook shots, I was in tune with my body, my essence; the communion with God was so easy. It was God, basketball, and me.

The mutuality, the team, the passing, the lay-up, late at night I would turn on a special lone light in the gym and have my best talks with God and oh, how I listened. There was no still small voice. The sound was BIG, yet soft like the SWISH.

In this upper-middle-class, predominantly white (except for international students) prep school with its ivy-covered brick buildings and manicured lawns, I met her. Yes, one day as I was entering the ivy-covered classroom building, the white wooden door swung open and there she was. Her dark eyes pierced into me, and I felt known like I felt when playing basketball. SWISH!

Her name was Annie, and in the days and weeks to follow I knew something so beautiful was happening to me, and in the evening playing basketball I talked with God about Annie — about the sacred feelings and connections I had with her. These connections were like knowing God, but in a deeper way. It was in that knowing that Sophia made herself known to me inside of me. I felt alive and free, ready to do and be me in a whole new way. God, basketball, Annie, and me.

As the weeks followed, I overheard friends talking about the two women who were seniors then. I noticed Bebe and Sally — that they too looked at one another in that knowing way. The way that made me tingle inside — like Annie and me. Then the talk began. The quiet whispers, a word I really hadn't heard before, "They are homosexual; they are dirty and bad." I began to whirl inside. What was this? What were others saying? In the weeks to follow Bebe and Sally were invited — yes, escorted out of our school.

The cacophony of sound outside — all the noise outside seeped into my insides and the sacred connection, the big sound, began to become smaller. I felt a sense of desperation. I couldn't feel or hear her in me, and I became suspect to myself. What I knew to be true was shattered, and I feared myself with Annie.

No longer going to the Presbyterian Church where I taught Sunday school to first-graders each week, but racing to the local Roman Catholic Church — in the quiet — the candles flickering, I prayed, "Oh, help me God. How can this be happening? How can anything so good be seen as wrong?" But the outward sounds snuffed out my inner ones, and it wasn't until I was thirty-eight that two little boys and their daddy coaxed me back to life again. The Swish sound came back into my life. Once again I could feel and hear. I could breathe deeply. I let Sophia God in again. SWISH. The deepest crevices shut off were healing. I was coming back, and with my lesbian self honored by my family I began to flourish. And surely as I am standing here before you, Sophia said to me, "Welcome home to yourself." And the church said, "Go away."

From that time onward Sophia has invited me into places and ministries I would never have dreamed possible.

When did God first visit you? When did you feel God deep inside and know her? What happens to us when God rises within and calls to us to come into the open air — to come to the city gates, to the highways and byways of our lives — calling us out into what is really going on, calling us forth to dig deeper?

In Alice Randall's *The Wind Done Gone,* a little girl is raised in slavery. The master who owned her taught her to read and write, traveled with her and took her everywhere. He was the one who schooled her, "his woman." She says this about him:

He wants to marry me. He asked me on bended knee and I would have to be honored except he wants us to live in London and he wants me to live white. I crowed at that, I laughed so hard not a tear came. He couldn't understand it. I don't often think on how white I look; it has always been a question of how colored I feel and I feel plenty colored. I said, "I am colored — I'm colored black — the way I talk, the way I look, the way I do most everything," but he said, "You don't have to be." At last that explained everything.

You've got to be in your skin to know. It is not only the pigment of my skin — no, it is not the color of my skin — it is the color of my mind, and my mind is dark and dusky, like a beautiful night. I cannot go to London and forget my color. I don't want to — not anymore.

Sophia Wisdom — the way of knowing she who is who calls us out through our pain, through the oppressive systems into new knowledge. It is tasting, touching, and feeling the freedom. It is the voice so small that grows louder and louder inside of us with our hearts racing until — out of the abuse, out, out, out.

"Simple fools, simple fools . . . these tears bring communities into healing and wholeness."

In the inner city of Pittsburgh, Pennsylvania, the city where I was raised, Wanda Graham Harris took this well-read, white, privileged woman and taught her firsthand about racism, classism, ageism, and sexism, from her social location. From the streets of Hazelwood in a "changing neighborhood," where hunger and poverty seeped under the doors, where violence lived outside and inside the homes, when absentee fathers and head of household mothers tried to raise their children in a system that was breaking up family and community. It was the city where I was raised. This was a different part of the city where I was told, "Don't go there; you will be hurt, you will be raped." But Evie Holmes, a neighbor, called me and said, "Don't tell your mother I told you, but there is an opening in Hazelwood and you ought to apply. Please do not tell your mother."

I was so glad to get that call. Women couldn't find jobs in ministry, hardly in Pittsburgh, where there are over three hundred Presbyterian churches. This was a nibble. Jim and our two sons, Jim and Chet, drove to Hazelwood in time to meet Wanda and her family dousing a fire around the garbage cans in the back of the church. "Kids were meddling in here," she yelled. "Come on in." My boys went to play with her sons, and Jim and I sat in her office as she told us about Hazelwood Presbyterian Ministry.

Here I met Sophia, in Hazelwood. "You know nothing about being poor — oh, you read about it, and you may think you know, but come with me." She took me to the streets, to the projects, to the schools. Side by side we worked through summer programs with black and white city youth on the streets and on retreats, praying from the deepest part of us. They called us the "checkerboard staff." After the third month, a note was slipped under my door. It read: "Welcome to my world, Janie Spahr." This reminded me of a saying, "If you come to help me, you are wasting your time. But if you have come because your liberation is bound up with mine, then let us work together."

And so we did. This naïve, liberal, white, privileged young mother and preacher went to graduate school in life experience. No longer naïve, sickened by how racism and classism devastate a community, we went to work. Wanda mentored me. "Always use your privilege for good."

When I was invited to become co-pastor of this wonderful church (Downtown United Presbyterian Church, Rochester, New York), and when I was denied and became an evangelist, I called Wanda. She said, "You know, Janie, I have been curriculum for the Presbyterian Church for thirty years. In the early years folks would come and ask if they could touch my hair." She asked me, "Are you called to be curriculum for the Presbyterian Church? If you are, then you should say 'yes'." And so I did.

I continue to be stunned by a Presbyterian Church that is so wrapped up in the Lordship of Jesus Christ that we forget the many ways, traditions, and cultures God comes to us through Sophia, who is the co-creator with God, she who moves in us, through us, and among us. Yes, Sophia shows up in the most unexpected places.

Sophia shows up crying out to a church that is rule-led rather than Spirit-fed.

She speaks, "When churches you participate in exclude lesbian, gay, bisexual, and transgender people from living their full selves, causing death, violence, and abuse . . . I will rise up within them and set them free — for they are my delight and you are messing with sacred mystery."

I am Sophia, the wisdom of God who created you. You cannot confine me.

I am the breath of the power of God.

Come into the open air. Come into the city streets, out of your comfortable church pews. Come find me in yourselves once again. Then see what kinds of worlds we will build together.

Sophia says, "The ball is in our court!"

I hear the SWISH. Can you hear her? Can you feel her? Can you feel you? Can you feel church? Listen!

SWISH, SWISH, SWISH

Analysis

Spahr's sermon based on exegesis of Proverbs employs Sophia as the feminine image of God. Not knowing what that might look like to the hearers, Spahr uses a basketball sound, "swish," as a common image or sound. Repeating the word "swish" in certain places creates an image in the mind of the listener of how Sophia, a more fluid image of God, might sound. Part narrative and part autobiography, Spahr's sermon invites the hearer to consider things we have pushed down or denied about our beings that might, in fact, hold the greatest truth for us. Consider Alice Randall's character "passing for white" but knowing deep within herself that she is black, that black is her state of mind and she can no longer pretend otherwise. Spahr highlights from Proverbs how Sophia shows up in unexpected places like the crossroads, portals, and the gates of the city. Sophia is not afraid to move around and call from various places. She is not so much concerned with right ways as she is with living ways. This is also what Jesus is trying to teach the disciples in Matthew 15. The religious ones are concerned with purity, eating with unclean hands, but Jesus says that is not the issue. It is what comes out of our mouths, out of our hearts that defiles us. Spahr questions how the Presbyterian Church, her church, continues to worry about purity and rule following, when the Head of the church, Jesus, was not. Prophetically Spahr proclaims that Sophia claims life for all people, including those who have formerly been excluded. Spahr describes Sophia as the God within and the God without. Sophia, meaning wisdom, is the God who knows us deeper than we know ourselves sometimes. And it is this God, Sophia, that helped her know herself as a lesbian woman. Sophia God is a feminine image of God who delights in LGBT people because she delights in who she has created. One might say Sophia comes out on behalf of sexual minorities. At the end, Spahr sets Sophia loose in the congregation with the sound and image of Swish, Swish, Swish.

&

The next homily is by Jay Emerson Johnson, programming and development director at the Center for Lesbian and Gay Studies in Religion and Ministry, and was preached in the Pacific School of Religion's chapel on National Coming Out Day, 2005. The biblical texts are woven throughout the sermon as it recalls various people of faith and their stories.

Sermon:
"GOD COMES OUT!"
by Jay Emerson Johnson

According to Genesis, the beauty and wonders of creation came out of a formless void.

Abraham, our ancient ancestor in faith, came out of his homeland and traveled to a distant, unknown country.

Abraham's descendants came out of their slavery in Egypt to a land of freedom, but only after coming out of their sojourn in the desert.

Many generations later, a handful of their descendants came out of an upper room where they had huddled together in fear behind locked doors. According to the book of Acts, their bold preaching of the gospel "turned the world upside down."

A religious zealot by the name of Saul came out of violent persecution to become Paul, an equally zealous missionary for the truly radical idea that Gentiles could be people of faith too.

Given the political and cultural climate of American society today, I think it's high time that God came out.

God has done it before, you know. God came out in the voices of ancient Hebrew prophets crying for justice and peace. God came out in the life of a Palestinian peasant girl called Mary, who declared God's favor on the outcast. God came out in Jesus of Nazareth, promising sight to the blind and release for the captives.

God came out in St. Francis of Assisi and Julian of Norwich; in Sojourner Truth and Walter Rauschenbusch; in Dorothy Day and Martin Luther King Jr. and in many, many others. And it's high time that God came out again.

As a gay man who's becoming a bit queer around the edges, I've come out before, more times than I care to count, and will likely do so many more times in the future. And it is never easy.

These days, especially here in the Bay Area, coming out as a Christian feels a lot more queer than who I happen to date. For that kind of coming out, I need help; I need the loving support of a community — and so also with God.

When Lazarus came out of the tomb he was still wrapped in burial linens. Jesus told his friends to unbind him.

Today God is bound and all wrapped up in the politics of fear, in the ideologies of division and in the machinations of war. It's high time God came out, unbound in bold preaching, in ministries of radical welcome and inclusion, and in fearless loving.

None of us can do this unbinding on our own. But together we can become a beacon of the God who refuses to remain in the closet.

In the words of Isaiah, the people who walked in darkness have seen a great light.

Dear people of God, that light is in each and every one of us.

Don't hide it. Let it out. Let it shine.

Amen.

Analysis

Johnson's sermon is more like a homily because of its informality, its popular and familiar conversational tone.[23] A homily is usually shorter in length, follows the Scripture reading, and leads into the sacrament of Communion. The homily appeals to contemporary culture by being attentive to the hearers on that particular day and in that particular context. For Johnson, that means National Coming Out Day on a seminary campus. This day is to encourage people who are afraid and still in the closet to consider coming out and living out. Johnson banks his message on all the times in Scripture that God and God's people have come out. In this way, the sermon is similar to Glaser's approach to the Bible as a source of coming out themes, yet, Johnson adds a unique twist. Being in his context that is supportive of LGBT

---

23. Wardlaw, "Homiletics and Preaching in North America," 258.

people, and being an out gay man, he turns the tables by asking for help in coming out as a Christian in his community. Living in Berkeley, California, one can imagine more tolerance for difference than for conformity, in this case Christianity. Johnson's message thus aims to invite hearers to consider the ways God has come out in the biblical narratives and for them to come out on God's behalf. Though short in words, Johnson's message is long on thoughts. It provides one with many different images from Scripture, each having to do with a "coming out." While it suggests to LGBT their coming out process, straight people can hear the text from a gay man's perspective too. Johnson is speaking to the hearers as Christians overshadowed by a larger Christian voice that claims power and privilege over others. This Christian voice ruins Jesus' message of radical inclusivity and discipleship. The homily includes all in the call to come out for God, meaning, I interpret, to speak up about God and Jesus in a climate that may be hostile to Christianity altogether. Religious practice, like one's sexuality, is unknown unless one speaks up and gives witness. Johnson invites us, on both accounts, to claim the God we know and person we are.

Both of these sermons fall into Paul Scott Wilson's category of "radical postmodern homiletics," as they strive to include the stranger and outsider without repeating suffering done to certain people and groups in society.[24] Both preachers are out lesbian and gay clergy who are preaching from that perspective. Their own experience of suffering as sexual minorities gives them the ability to understand the suffering of others. Spahr does this when she includes the experience of a person of color who knows her color and delights in it even though being white might give her more privilege in society. Johnson does this when he claims to know that coming out as a Christian in Berkeley and other places is just as hard as coming out as a sexual minority, but he

---

24. Paul Scott Wilson, *Preaching and Homiletical Theory* (St. Louis: Chalice Press, 2004), 145.

encourages it anyway. Together these preachers call hearers to enlarge their image and practice of God.

This chapter concludes with many avenues to what a lesbian or gay God looks like and what that means theologically. Not having one particular idea or image could be disappointing. Yet there is not one image, nor one coming out, for there are and will be many more. Like most theological movements, this one includes church voices from the past, current scholarly work, parish ministers and the laity, and perspectives from the culture at large, mixed in with individual personal experience of being a lesbian, gay, bisexual, or transgender person of faith. The homiletical task involves listening to these strands of thought about the meaning of queer life in the church. Out LGBT preachers and our straight allies are the mouthpieces that name the queer God. As LGBT people, we embody this God as we speak about the divine, the holy Other, in ways that seem normal in our lives, but come across as just a bit odd or strange to our hearers. In this exchange, God comes out, thus freeing all of us from preconceived notions about sexuality in relation to God. From a healthier sexuality that acknowledges the sacred, we are able to move toward healing this crisis of sexuality in our church, and hopefully in the culture.

Chapter 7

Coming Home

My hope is that in the course of this book, and perhaps particularly the sermons, you have recognized that out gay and lesbian preachers and their allies bring a unique homiletical voice, hermeneutical method, and theology to the field of homiletics and to the church as a whole. By coming out to ourselves and to our vocational call to ministry, we have come home to God. The notion of "coming home to God" is a descriptive way of speaking personally about one's sense of belonging. For those of us who found our home in God, but were exiled when being true to our deepest being — lesbian, gay, bisexual, or transgender — did not coincide with those who represented God, who served in the church, and who preached condemning words, coming home is a profound experience. Describing this himself, Bishop Gene Robinson likens his "coming home" experience to the prodigal son's return home.

> I feel like the Prodigal Son, you know. God has given me all these gifts, and I have, I am sure, squandered many of them in a far-off realm. But I am trying to get back home. I am probably not going to get there before I am dead and gone, but what I can be assured of is that God will come running toward me with his arms outstretched, and before I can utter "I am sorry," God will be putting a robe on me and a ring on my finger and ordering up a party. That's what I really believe. So I don't have to be sure about any one verse or any one story. I could be wrong. But I don't believe that my salvation depends on it, because my

salvation has already been won. All I have to do is accept it, and then do my very best to be God's hands and feet in the world.[1]

This God welcomes him with open arms and a party, celebrating that he has returned home. Would that the church could imitate this God in response to LGBT people! There would be many a party. The parallel used here is not meant to interpret LGBT people as squandering their inheritance as the prodigal son did; rather, it is used to show how God responds to those who come seeking home. Coming home to God is also an expression used to describe our coming out experience in spiritual terms. Coming out is always about saying "yes" to ourselves and to our sexuality, which is at the very core of our being — our desires, affections, and longings, as persons made in the image of God. Coming out is also about a fuller understanding of sexuality and thereby God's coming out of the straight closet. It is this coming out that brings an opportunity for a fuller understanding of the way God is known to us. Ultimately, the purpose of preaching is to bring God out of the closet of our spiritual lives and into action within our community. In our best efforts, whenever we preach and with the Spirit's guidance, God comes out.

Preaching by LGBT clergy and allies mends the torn fabric of sexuality and community in the church. Even more, our preaching is bringing God out of the closet and loosening the grip of heterosexism. It is an expression of not only the freedom we can and should feel in the pulpit as preachers, but also the freedom of those in the pew. As Gene Bartlett writes about preaching:

The Protestant tradition therefore rests upon two freedoms, not one. There is the freedom of the pulpit in which the congregation cannot tell the preacher what he must preach, or what he may not. But there is also the freedom of the pew in which the minister may neither require the assent nor prohibit the dissent of the

---

1. Gene Robinson, "Scripture and Homosexuality," *Tikkun* (July 2006): 21, excerpted from Elizabeth Adams, *Going to Heaven: The Life and Election of Bishop Gene Robinson* (Brooklyn, NY: Soft Skull Books, 2006).

worshiper. Between these two freedoms, we believe there is ample room for the gift of God's Word to come with freshness and power.[2]

The freedom in the pew allows people to hear and respond to preaching as led by God. Beyond a certain point, the preacher cannot control what a person receives from either the preacher's physical presence in the pulpit or the sermon itself. Who I am as a child of God, created in God's image — my whole being — is reflected in the preaching event, even though my sermons do not directly deal with the nature of my sexual orientation. As Bartlett rightly states, it is between these two freedoms that the Holy Spirit works in our preaching and in the listeners' lives.

Curious about my experience of preaching as an out lesbian, I wondered how other out preachers were faring in their pulpits. Through a survey sent to LGBT clergy and our straight allies, I received input that tested my theory. It went to a sampling of preachers, to friends who knew of a friend's pastor, and e-mail lists from Witness Our Welcome (a multidenominational gathering of persons from Open and Affirming/Welcoming congregations) and the United Church of Christ Coalition for Gay and Lesbian Concerns. Of the one hundred surveys sent out, just under half were returned.

These forty-six responses by LGBT and straight clergy identify how these preachers are heard differently and thus shape a homiletic that reflects the lived experience of clergy. These clergy are in ministries that include hospital and hospice chaplaincy, seminary teaching, parish ministry, pulpit supply preaching, and being an interim pastor and camp director. Nineteen are from UCC pastors; fifteen of those are in ONA congregations and four in other recognized ministerial settings. Only two of the nineteen UCC pastors were not out professionally in their ministry context. Three of the surveys returned are from Metropolitan Community Church clergy who are out and practice their ministry in churches that are 97 percent LGBT. Nine surveys are from clergy in the Episcopal Church, Presbyterian Church

---

2. Gene E. Bartlett, *The Audacity of Preaching: The Lyman Beecher Lectures* (New York: Harper & Brothers, 1962), 46.

(USA), United Methodist Church, Disciples of Christ, American Baptist Church, and the Evangelical Lutheran Church in America. Most of these clergy are not out in these churches because denominational policies prevent them from doing so and retaining their ordination. Their churches remain open to LGBT people, but they have not formally voted on a welcoming statement. The fifteen straight clergy allies are known in their congregations and denominations for their support of clergy who are same-gender-loving.

From the results, I draw these observations: first, gay or lesbian clergy who are at ONA churches with a majority heterosexual congregation are perceived to be preaching about homosexuality more than those who are at churches with a majority population of lesbian, gay, bisexual, and transgender members (MCC). Surprisingly, one respondent, who ministers in an MCC church, said, "People complain that I preach too much on gay issues, but there is never any agreement on what is too much or not enough." Even in a predominantly lesbian and gay church, listeners perceive the preacher to be preaching about gay issues while the preacher does not see it that way. Due to the relatively new position of out clergy preaching, perhaps this newness of lesbian and gay clergy has not worn off, and listeners hear our sexuality louder than they would if they had been listening to out clergy for twenty years.

Second, if a gay or lesbian clergyperson is not out, but the church is ONA or welcoming, then there is less conflict over what he or she preaches. In other words, being in the closet prevents people from hearing "sexual identity" in their sermons. These respondents who are not out, but are serving in ONA congregations, reported not preaching on LGBT topics (probably out of fear of being outed) and said that the perception from the congregation's view is accurate — that they don't think their preacher preaches too much about LGBT people.

Third, the majority of out gay or lesbian clergy and straight allies believed their preaching was well received unless they had specific references to homosexual issues. For those preachers who included something in their sermons about LGBT people and did not make it "an issue," the message carried more weight and fewer complaints. For example, a reference to a lifelong partnership between two men or women is typically received better if made without using descriptive words like "homosexuals" or "gay." One generally gets a better response by preaching a sermon like the one on Harry and Herman's anniversary than if one were to preach about "gay marriage rights." In other words, a relational (I-Thou) approach by using names and personal lives of people who are also lesbian and gay gives more dimension and reality and will usually be received well. By avoiding labels and facing the full humanity of queer people, the church begins to live its faith in Jesus the Christ. Priest and professor Barbara Brown Taylor writes eloquently about the problem of labels:

> The problem I run into (at the bakery) is that I do not have a *position* on homosexuality. What I have, instead, is a life. I have a history, in which many people have played vital parts. When I am presented with the *issue* of homosexuality, I experience temporary blindness. Something like scales fall over my eyes, because I cannot visualize an *issue*. Instead, I visualize the homeroom teacher who seemed actually to care whether I showed up at school or not. I see the priest who taught me everything I know about priesthood, and the professor who roasted whole chickens for me when my food money ran out before the end of the month. I see the faces of dozens of young men who died of AIDS, but not before they had shown me how brightly they could burn with nothing left but the love of God to live on.[3]

The "problem" as Taylor sees it is that others expect a position regarding homosexuality rather than seeing people for who they are, which is what I hear Buber saying in his I-Thou theology. Rev. Taylor describes people in her life who have taught her, fed her, cared for her, and loved her. Their sexual orientation is not what matters; it

---

3. Barbara Brown Taylor, "Where the Bible Leads Me," Faith Matters, *Christian Century*, October 18, 2003.

is the quality of relationship between the people involved. Essentially this is what preaching is — to speak as one human being to another of things sacred and holy.

Fourth, straight clergy preaching about LGBT people or issues related to our presence are challenged by members of their congregations. A straight clergyperson coming out, as Thomas Troeger and Susan Sumwalt-Patterson did in their sermons, opens up the possibility that they will lose some of their power with those who disagree with their stance of support for LGBT people. Straight clergy who do not mention LGBT people in their sermons, but do support us outside of the pulpit, like in social action or pastoral counseling, received no negative feedback from their congregations. This, of course, is not true in every straight preacher ally setting. There were some references to sermons from straight people making more impact than those from an openly gay person, if the congregation is struggling about these things.

In response to the question, "Is the perception of how often you preach/write/teach on LGBT issues accurate?" one MCC pastor noted something unusual; he wrote, "People in our congregation tend to discount the importance of simply preaching as an openly gay person." This pastor is speaking from within an LGBT congregation and thinks the members do not realize that his very presence sends a message, even before he opens his mouth to preach. They seem to have forgotten the tension between the church and the LGBT world — the assumed scriptural injunctions against homosexuality. His presence in the pulpit has thus grown comfortable for them. In research thus far it seems that, knowingly or unknowingly, an openly lesbian or gay preacher sends a message simply by her or his presence that is interpreted as the preacher "talking about 'it' too much" — meaning talking about sexuality and specifically lesbian or gay sexuality. Therefore, churches need further awareness about their heterosexual privileges. For example, in an answer to the same question ("Is the perception of how often you preach/write/teach on LGBT issues accurate?") a lesbian clergy wrote, "No, there is a sense that I preach on 'it' far more often than I really do." She serves a UCC church that has a growing lesbian, gay, bisexual, and transgendered population of 14 percent in her congregation. She has the task of involving the increasing number of LGBT members with the majority and typically straight longtime members. This is hard work because it is frontier work — entering into the new territory of lesbian and gay preachers being called to congregations that are primarily heterosexual. As more churches decide to become part of the Welcoming Movement, the possibility of calling an out LGBT person is higher, and these instances will likely increase. As lesbian and gay preachers preach and congregations welcome them into the pulpit, they will build authentic community by looking, listening, touching, feeling, seeking, and finding where God is coming out among us.

When God comes out through the preaching of a lesbian, gay, or straight clergyperson, the sermon will take many different forms, as illustrated in the ten sermons included in this work. There is no one sermon method (such as inductive, narrative, or conversational preaching) that works best for a gay and lesbian homiletic, but the hallmarks of a lesbian and gay homiletic provide guidelines. The ten sermons included in this book are different as people are different. In general, though, it is a homogeneous group of preachers who are in widely different contexts. While more diversity among the preachers regarding race, class, creed, and economic status is needed, the focus here is on lesbian and gay sexual orientation. On the sexual orientation scale, the preachers run the gamut: two sermons are by straight clergy, four sermons by out lesbian clergy, one by a closeted lesbian, one by a closeted clergyman, and two by out gay men. Including a sermon by a closeted clergywoman represents the location of many clergy who cannot afford to come out of the closet and maintain their ministerial license due to denominational policy. Whether one agrees with the practice of ministry from within the closet is not the question; it is the reality of life, and that must be respected. Including the sermon of a clergyman who is in the process of becoming aware of his sexual orientation as different from the one he was living yields yet another truth. It reminds us that while sexual orientation other than heterosexual can be denied for a time, it invariably comes to the surface at some point and one has the choice to recognize and deal with it or not. Preaching while in the midst of coming out is a challenging and vulnerable place. One's truth meets the truth of the gospel dwelling within us and delivers a reality that can be liberating and confounding at the same time. Remembering that truth comes through personality, the preacher's social location in life matters as much as, if not more than, the particular preaching method. Naming truth in the situation without naming it specifically (homosexual/lesbian/gay) allows the hearers to come to their own truth. This same approach seemed to work in Rev. Landis's sermon (chapter 4). He did not name his truth but encouraged others to explore and live their truth. Smith's sermon (chapter 4) directly named the violence toward LGBT people. She uses an example of a gay man's experience to read the gospel text. The straight preachers, Troeger and Sumwalt-Patterson, explicitly name gay and lesbian people in their sermons in ways that offer God's blessing. Sermons given in ONA or similar truth-telling contexts (Geslin, Smith, Hinnant, Plunder, Spahr, and Johnson) by out lesbians and gay men, moved into deeper theological realms and were not advertisements about sexuality or sex. Being out and being in an open congregation, preaching does not become all about human sexuality, as some have feared. Preaching by out LGBT clergy remains about the gospel and the fundamentals of Christian living. All of the sermons but one drew from New Testament texts, specifically the Gospels and most from Luke. Another interesting note about this collection of sermons is that parables were used frequently as a means of teaching — as Jesus used them with his disciples, and whose meaning still teaches disciples today. One reason parables are used often in preaching from, by, or about LGBT people and our allies is that parables, like riddles, have a way of bringing the hearer into the lived example, inviting them to respond and learn for themselves. This approach, somewhat like an inductive method, allows the readers to come to terms with God's grace and truth as they are able and ready. It does not define for others specifically what the answer should be, but raises up a range of possibilities in response to life. An interesting study might be a survey of biblical texts used most often in sermons by LGBT clergy and on our behalf. As the number of closeted and out LGBT clergy grows, a collection of our sermons would reveal core Scripture, hermeneutical interpretations, and theological basis, all contributing further to an LGBT homiletic.

Throughout this book, terms, labels, and definitions about sexual orientation have been used for identification and investigation. Using labels to define a person is both inadequate and incomplete. Naming a person as lesbian or gay is only an aspect of their being. However, to create a homiletic, it has been necessary to examine the concerns and characteristics of this minority group living in a majority culture. In chapter 1, Martin E. Marty wished we could begin again with the I-Thou dialogue — instead of I-It. Through this homiletic, we have begun again by relating to one another as fully alive human beings engaged in God's ongoing revelation. Preachers play a major role in shaping practical, lived theology in churches through their sermons and ministry. Thus, it is necessary to seek a homiletic that engages with lesbians, gay men, bisexuals, transgendered people, and/or "queers" in relation to our experience of coming out, the Bible, theology, sermons, sexuality, and Christian living. This lesbian and gay homiletic needs to be continually shaped by the experience of LGBT clergy in welcoming churches and unwelcoming churches as we learn what preaching means from these vistas.

This book is only a beginning. Though I don't have firm evidence, I confidently believe that lesbian and gay preachers will continue serving congregations where their sexual orientation is in the minority (except if serving the Universal Fellowship of Metropolitan Community Churches, a queer church) and that we will continue learning how this shapes our churches and our task of preaching. My hope is that it will prompt many more discussions and many more sermons on the topic of such preaching, and encourage clergy and laity to do this work of giving us glimpses of God coming out in pulpits everywhere.

Biblical Index

General Index